MODERN AMERICAN PAINTING

MODERN AMERICAN PAINTING

By PEYTON BOSWELL, JR.

EDITOR OF "THE ART DIGEST"

WITH EIGHTY-NINE ILLUSTRATIONS IN FULL COLOR SELECTED FROM THE
SERIES ON CONTEMPORARY AMERICAN ARTISTS PUBLISHED IN "LIFE"

New York
DODD, MEAD & COMPANY
1940

MODERN AMERICAN PAINTING

FOREWORD

Credit Where It Is Due

A NEW AND POWERFUL INSTRUMENT has been placed at the service of American art. When C. Powell Minnegerode, director of the Corcoran Gallery, sent the following telegram to Henry Luce, congratulating *Life* on its "Pageant of America" series of contemporary painting commissions, he expressed the overwhelming opinion of the entire American art world. Said Mr. Minnegerode: "*Life's* commissioning of these paintings is a further step in the program of art education which, over the past two years, has made *Life* the most significant single force in the appreciation of art in America." Corcoran's director had put into words the thoughts of all of us who, through the years, have labored to do in our small circumscribed area what *Life* is doing on a national scale.

This volume, dedicated to America's new school of native painting, was possible only because of *Life's* deep interest in the growth of American art appreciation and the fact that its editors had sagaciously recognized the presence of an authentic American School even before it became the vital movement it is today. *Life*, as one more contribution to the cause of American Art, has very generously made available to the publishers of *Modern American Painting* the beautiful full-color plates which in the following pages herald the coming-of-age of art in the New World.

All except one of the paintings reproduced in this book are, therefore, a selection from *Life's* fine continuing series on American artists and it would not have been possible to present these expensive engravings for so moderate a price had not *Life* made its plates available in book form.

With its circulation of more than 2,300,000, *Life* is doing a remarkable job of art education. This has never been done on such a scale before. Under the banner of Henry Luce, and his associates and assistants, this work of carrying appreciation and knowledge of art to the far corners of the land has been wisely guided. The eventual effect of such mass-impact of art upon the dormant sensitivities of an entire nation, like the Government's entry into art patronage, cannot help but react to the greater health of American art. *Life* has widened the circle.

Following the principal text of this book, the reader will find, arranged in alphabetical order, biographies of each of the artists and comments about the paintings that are reproduced here. At the end there is included a Catalogue of Paintings where, together with other data, are listed the galleries and owners to whom I am greatly indebted for their kind permission to reproduce these paintings.

I want at this point to express my appreciation for the valuable collaboration rendered this book by artist Margit Varga, of *Life*, who wrote the biographies of the artists whose work is reproduced, and who shares with me an unbounded faith and enthusiasm for modern American painting.

PEYTON BOSWELL, JR.

To "P.B."
(My Father)

CONTENTS

The Text

The Paintings

CONTENTS

The Paintings

CONTENTS

The Paintings

MODERN AMERICAN PAINTING

AMERICA today is developing a School of Painting which promises to be the most important movement in the world of art since the days of the Italian Renaissance. Never in the nation's history has there been a time when art was so widely appreciated or so seriously practiced as it is today. America salutes the past, and is grateful to Europe for the aesthetic problems it has solved for all nations. But to this technical knowledge we have now added something that is entirely our own—our own way of life, our own way of thinking and feeling, or our American spirit, if you want to give this something its most inclusive meaning. As a result, the world is witnessing the birth of a new school of painting—the American School.

America waited three hundred years. Through three centuries American Art was a tantalizing promise, a vague hint of something more authentic than the imported culture from Europe's ateliers. Here and there through our history a solitary figure rose to indicate the art that might have been. But America could not understand these earlier native painters. It is only in this generation that Americans can lay claim to an art that expresses their feelings, thoughts and aspirations.

A major difference between Homer, Ryder and Eakins and such present-day painters as Hopper, Mattson and Brook is that the contemporaries have the good fortune to live in an age that wants to understand them. America now, mature and flushed with the pride of national strength, demands an art of her own. It was not thus when Copley traded his honest Yankee birthright for the frills of George III's London, or the lonely Ryder painted his gems in a dirty New York garret. Our painters have discovered America. And America has discovered her painters.

Today America need no longer dwell in Europe's house and live with Europe's art. America, in art, as in material progress, has a native spirit. How well our contemporary artists express that spirit can be seen from the reproductions in this book. After the post war era of international hysteria, our artists found the encouragement at home that they had needed for three hundred years. Europe was the cat that ate eleven billion canaries, but America emerged with a more precious possession—a true native art.

Nationalism, robust and sometimes ruthless, made this authentic American School flower. Only when our artists began to explore the highways and byways of their own land did their art take on the earthy fragrance of their native soil.

Grant Wood is one of these artists who came home to learn. Wood as a student in the Latin Quarter of Paris floundered among the "neo-meditationalists" who believed in waiting very quietly for inspiration. "And they did most of their waiting," Wood says, "at the Café Dome, or the Rotonde, with brandy. It was then that I realized that all the really good ideas I'd ever had came to me while I was milking a cow. So I went back to Iowa."

The same thing happened to Benton. After a quarter-century of trying to find himself in Paris and New York, he discovered he could best express himself in his home state of Missouri. "In New York," said Benton, "there are so many people living off ideas instead of really doing something. Too much of intellectual life is dominated by ideas that have never had a practical test. Things which are purely ideas are taken for realities and the intellectuals don't seem to be able to make the distinction. . . . The mule is a damned dramatic animal."

Curry was about to give up painting when, as a last resort, he painted a nostalgic scene of his childhood and called it *Baptism in Kansas.* This brought him immediate fame, and he returned to the Middle West to paint his own experiences in his own environment. "The artist," says Curry, "ought to paint people doing things. The use of life as an excuse for clever arrangements of color ends where it begins. If you feel the significance of life, the design builds itself. The feeling inherent in the life of the world cannot be ignored or trifled with for the sake of a theory."

This "return to the soil" extends even to the concrete pavements of our cities. Reginald Marsh, after years of experimenting in foreign isms, now paints New York because it is New York that arouses the deepest emotion in him. "My first subjects," says Marsh, "were construction workers, and French modernism offered little to show how to construct a man who was a man of bone and muscle. In other words, contemporary French aesthetic nuances, so attractively and widely ballyhooed, had to be brushed aside in order to study works of more substance."

And so it is with all our truly American painters. They have come home. The lessons these artists learned through bitter experience are being transmitted in our art schools to the youngsters who will be the headliners of tomorrow. The American tradition is bound to continue for years to come.

Art students who have been abroad hasten to explain that they went merely to visit, not to copy their European cousins. The public schools have awakened to the need for art. More and more colleges are installing the position of artist-in-residence, which means that a prominent artist is engaged to live on the campus, not to teach formal classes but to inspire the students by bringing them into actual contact with art in the making. Grant Wood holds this position at the University of Iowa; John Steuart Curry is at Wisconsin; Paul Sample at Dartmouth; and Lamar Dodd at Georgia, to mention but a few.

Art is so important to Americans that it transcends politics. Frick, Morgan, Mellon, Huntington plundered Europe's treasures for great art now available in museums. America's store of ancient art is large and surprisingly good. In the last ten years the great Whitney and Rockefeller fortunes have been thrown in the scale for modern art. Add to all this the vastly important assistance of the Federal government, which has spent more than $19,000,000 during the past five years to encourage the native painter and to bring *original* art before the masses of Americans. And at the same time art interest has greatly increased among the people, as shown by the growing attendance at museums and galleries, the fact that upwards of 35,000 artists, craftsmen and designers are working at their professions, and that literally hundreds of art schools are overflowing with students—youngsters who no longer feel the need of European instruction. Within the last quarter century, while the population has gained slightly less than 25 per cent, there has been a more than 300 per cent increase in the number of art museums, art schools, art societies and professional artists.

Modern American painting is a vast movement. There are 20,000 active artists in the United

States today. Of these it is safe to say that two hundred are doing work of real significance. Hundreds of young recruits are coming up every year from the nation's five hundred art schools.

This new movement has often been referred to as an American Renaissance. But to be reborn before birth would indeed be an obstetrical miracle. A better word for the movement is "naissance." Art in America is a creative flowering of today. It is an art indigenous to its environment, an insoluble compound of America's spirit and its people. It is a new school of taste in the world's art.

Discovery of an Artistic Nationality

In America, the artist has once again accomplished his historic mission—for Art is the cultural expression of the human race in visual terms, just as, by the same token, Science is the culture of a people expressed in terms of applied experiment to the *how* of things, and Philosophy is culture expressed in terms of reasoning into the *why* of things. Music fills the same function in terms of sound, and Literature in terms of the written language.

Art is perhaps the oldest of any of these modes of expression. While still a savage, man started to express beauty in the things he created. He gave line and balance to his first rude instruments. As he progressed, stage by stage, in the long journey from brute to civilized man, so did his tendency to feel and express, but—and here may be found the secret of the new American School—he always felt parochially and he always expressed his parochialism ultimately in terms of nationalism.

America is not a race, but a people. By the mingling of the bloods of many races we have developed a native school or taste (they mean the same) in painting. American art is not an ethnological, but a sociological product. America, composed of many races, has welded those races into a national unity; into a people held together by the unbreakable ties of common interests, communal characteristics, the same national spirit and the same love of liberty. Within its borders all races are one people, each contributing to the national character. And it is largely because of this larger national spirit, this inner unity of complex racial strains, that America has at last evolved an art able to express the thoughts and feelings of her people.

From this national spirit has sprung the art that stirs us so deeply today. What makes an American is not necessarily the blood of his fathers but the American spirit with which he reacts to American society. The latest canvases of German-born George Grosz, although he has been in this country only a few years, bear the imprint of this spirit; the paintings of American-born Lionel Feininger, on the other hand, are almost pure German expressionism. It is not the subject alone that makes an American painting. Neither is it the technique, for technique in painting is an international bequest, passed down from one age to the next, modified to the national needs of the peoples who use it. It is, rather, through the spirit or feeling with which technique is applied that our national traits emerge in the paintings of our artists.

An artist who capitalizes on the lessons of the Old World, and at the same time feels America as he paints her—to him we affix the label "American," whether he be a Waldo Peirce, who employs the impressionist technique to paint Maine family life and country fairs, or a Walt Kuhn, who blends the French modernism of Cézanne and Derain with the Greek classic and studies life on city streets or in the sawdust ring of a circus. These, we claim, "paint American" along with such "American

Sceners" as Charles Burchfield, Grant Wood, John Steuart Curry, Thomas Benton, James Chapin, Reginald Marsh, Alexandre Hogue and others long affiliated with native subject matter.

Others who have *adopted* European technique without *adapting* it to the national spirit—artists like the late Allen Tucker, who worshiped Van Gogh; John Marin, master technician, who paints Maine and New Mexico much as he would Brittany or Savoy; Stuart Davis, who abstracts with a decided French accent; Max Weber, master colorist, disciple of Cézanne; Maurice Sterne, Marsden Hartley, Charles Demuth and Arthur Dove—these we hail as fine artists, but not as "American" artists; they are the remnant of the once powerful international contingent.

The trend in American painting today—and I predict its future—is to blend the literal art of what we commonly term the "American Scene" with the lessons of modern aesthetics, to give greater attention to texture, color and relationship of forms. Our painting remains a literal, three-dimensional art, but Americans are assimilating the fundamentals of modernism.

When a scientist undertakes to build a new, revolutionary engine, he does not arbitrarily discard all that man has discovered about engines since Cecil first caused wheels to revolve through internal combustion. Rather, he goes on from where others stopped. That is what we have done in American art—gone on to a union of old and modern forces.

Nationalism, bred of disillusionment with international entanglements during the World War, is the prime cause behind the development of the new school of American painting—the only new development today in the world of art.

From all history, it is evident that the emergence of a native American art today has proceeded from a logical course of events.

After material conquest comes leisure, and with leisure follow art, music, literature. In the economically significant years of America's development, when its people were struggling against the forces of nature—some to drive westward the frontier; some to make the soil yield subsistence; some to refine raw materials into manufactured products, invent means of communication and transportation —the minds of men were given over to material problems that left little room for an interest in beauty. A tree was an obstruction to agriculture, a river was an avenue of transportation, an Indian was a barrier to advancing civilization.

A people struggling against primeval nature for survival grew to regard material things, things of flesh comfort, as all-important. Houses were built for the same reason as boxes, to contain something; beauty in the home and beauty in the mind were not essentials. When an individual, through exceptional energy or courage, forced his head above his fellows economically he could readily buy or copy from Europe what he desired, from Victorian morals to rococo carvings or classic domes for his state capitals. This materialism of America, our foreign pandering contemporaries say, has stamped itself indelibly on the national character. At any rate, it has caused contempt to be expressed by the internationalists and shame to be felt by Americans.

Several years have passed, however, since materialism ceased to obstruct the cultural growth of America. By this I do not advance the happy belief that America has been cleansed of its traditional "bad taste." We still have about us much convincing evidence to the contrary; our radios blare forth the syncopated bones of the great composers; our highways are desecrated by the commercialized vice of outdoor advertising; our towns and cities have the shabby, temporary appearance of a population about to move out *en masse*; the bulk of our people still decorate their homes with department-store color reproductions and obtain their literary diet from confessions of unrequited love or murder-rape-divorce-spiced tabloids.

But while we admit the truth of these accusations, let us not forget that America has more art museums than any other nation, and probably more practicing artists, designers and architects. Europe, in damning American taste, forgets that not long after Dickens turned a vitriolic pen against everything American, a booted Denver audience paid the most sincere of tributes to Oscar Wilde (the poet, not the man), and Texans named a town after the lovely voice of Lillie Langtry, the toast of Prince Edward's London. That was many years ago. Denver, built on the mineral wealth of the Rockies, is now a modern metropolis, proud of its art museum and other cultural advantages. Texas, vast in size and resources, boasts a host of good art museums, has incorporated art in the curricula of most of its many colleges and supports active art colonies in Dallas, Houston, San Antonio, and Fort Worth.

In the summer of 1938 occurred an event that supplied convincing evidence of our new national unity in art taste—the exhibition of American art which the Museum of Modern Art assembled for the Jeu de Paume Musée in Paris. The exhibits were carefully winnowed for presentation at the court of our former influences. Much depended on the verdict of that remarkably well-adjusted unit of French economy, the Parisian art critic. Would it be thumbs up or thumbs down? The decision was anxiously awaited by the American art world. Then came the transatlantic flash: it was thumbs down. The French critics liked our horseless carriages, our motion pictures, our bathtubs, but our art—Ah! Americans have no sensitivity; they should buy, not create. The sigh of relief that went up may have added slightly to the force of the hurricane that whipped along the Eastern seaboard that September. Had our art suited the French taste, it would not yet have been American.

The cat was unbagged by the exceptions the critics made in their general condemnation—the expatriates, Sargent, Whistler, Cassatt, old gods in our artistic hall of fame, who have been cellarized as national artistic conscience deepened. What did they mean to American art? The odor of the native soil had long been dissipated from their brushes. Sargent, born in Italy, worked, lived, died and is buried in England; Whistler lived and worked in England and his remains now lie in Chiswick Cemetery, London, beside the mother whose portrait is the most American picture he ever painted; Mary Cassatt, wealthy Philadelphia friend of Degas, spent her life in France and died in her chateau at Mesnil-Beaufresne, advising Americans to study at home. Homer, Ryder, Eakins are the masters to whom today's artists look.

We sense today the tension of that exciting moment when something cataclysmic is happening; we suspect rather than know the climax of a new phase in our national existence. In the following pages I hope to help define the meaning of that phase, an extremely reckless undertaking for a contemporary eyewitness without the advantages of tomorrow's perspective. To give this book a better semblance of order, the 89 full-color reproductions have been rather arbitrarily arranged in the following divisions: "Historical Ancestors," "American Scene," "Social Protest," and what, for want of a better term, we label "Pure Painting." Inclusion of a painting in any of these divisions does not necessarily mean that the artist belongs definitely in that category; rather it means that the particular canvas selected for reproduction fits best within one of these divisions. At first glance, the 68 reproductions of contemporary American paintings form a bewildering mosaic of art today, but with the possible exception of certain borderline examples—such as Peter Blume, Georgia O'Keeffe and Ralston Crawford —they represent essential elements in the new American School of painting. They paint a complete picture of American art as it is today.

Our Historical Ancestors

Art in America is less than 300 years of age. World art began about 4000 B.C., but possibly traces back 20,000 years, when our primitive forefathers first recorded their memoirs in caves in Spain and France and Central Africa—paintings and flint-drawings that have much of beauty and resemble the "art" of some prehistoric Paul Klee. Some scientists tell us that the Earth is two billion years old and, if they are correct, then the known history of mankind reaches back only an infinitesimal space— as measured by these drawings, the only records we have of those remote times. Everything else has perished. Art, through all the ages, has been the most expressive, most permanent thing in the lives of men. Almost all we know of the truly ancient nations—such as Egypt, Old China, Old India, Babylonia and Assyria—has been imparted to us through art. Of Greece and Rome, one of our best sources of information as to their real life, their thoughts, their religions is the work of their artists.

Ramses of Old Egypt is known to us through the artists who sculptured him in bas-relief when he was conquering western Asia. Tutankhamen was a dust-laden name until Egyptologists found his tomb and unearthed from it many examples of the art founded by his father-in-law, the heretic king Akhnaton, who rejected Ammon for Aton, a gentler god, and whose hymns to Aton were taken verbatim by the Jews into the Psalms of David. Old China, conquered many times but each time conquering her conqueror by absorption, exists for us today because of her philosophers, her poets and, most of all, her painters and sculptors.

And so it has been through all the pages of history, even in young America—as was dramatically demonstrated by the "Life in America" exhibition at the Metropolitan Museum in the summer of 1939. After passing through the museum's galleries, the visitor—perhaps confused by the nervous strain of contemporary living—emerged with the feeling that he had seen America in perspective, had been drenched in the redolence of the land and had tasted, to quote Hermann W. Williams, Jr., of the museum staff, "the substantial pork and beans of America, not its soufflés and meringues."

That exhibition, following the traditional American thread of realism and unveiling the natural parents of today's "American Scenism," summed up much of the history that will be retold in the following pages. Each of the 300 exhibits was a factual recording of a person, episode, or scene of actuality in the cavalcade of America. There were no studio nudes, no Greek mythologies, no soaring flights of the artistic spirit catapulted from some allegorical meeting of goddesses. But there were flights of spirit springing from more than one realistic view of American life.

Since to understand today and tomorrow it is essential to know yesterday, the reproductions in this book start logically with a section devoted to our American artist-ancestors. These examples by past Americans were selected to give as broad a view as possible of our artistic background, and they lead the reader by subsequent steps to the contemporary section, beginning with John Sloan, famous member of "The Eight" revolters for the new realism at the turn of the present century.

Benjamin West, pioneer internationalist, first of great artist-teachers and successor of Sir Joshua

The Death of Wolfe—Benjamin West

The Surrender of Lord Cornwallis—John Trumbull

Emigrant Train—SAMUEL COLMAN

Daniel Boone Escorting a Band of Pioneers into the Western Country—GEORGE CALEB BINGHAM

General Doubleday Crossing the Potomac—DAVID G. BLYTHE

Placer Mining—CHADWICK

Boston Harbor: Long and Central Wharves—ROBERT W. SALMON

Old Kentucky Home—Eastman Johnson

The Verdict of the People—George Caleb Bingham

Peace and

Max Schmitt in a Single Scull—THOMAS EAKINS

Death on a Pale Horse—ALBERT PINKHAM RYDER

The Little White Girl—JAMES MCNEILL WHISTLER

Prisoners from the Front—WINSLOW HOMER

The Gulf Stream—WINSLOW HOMER

Reynolds to the presidency of the Royal Academy in London, was the most vital link Colonial and Revolutionary Americans had with the art of the Mother Country. John Trumbull, greatest of the early artist-patriots, soldier and politician, painted such historical subjects as *The Surrender of Lord Cornwallis* (Page 17) because of his desire to inculcate in his fellow Americans love of country and liberty—an ambition that suffered from following too closely the traditional melodramatics of West's grand style. A generation later came such factual painter-reporters as George Caleb Bingham, David G. Blythe, Samuel Colman, Eastman Johnson and Robert W. Salmon, who depicted everyday views of life in the new nation as the March of Empire continued westward. George Inness, who marked the culmination of the misnamed Hudson River School which lost itself in the vastnesses west of the Mississippi, was the greatest of our early landscapists, one of the few Americans to paint with light and an original artist who might have founded a true American school had it not been for a too strong admiration of the French Barbizon painters.

The realistic strain, which is the most consistent thread woven through our American painting, finds, according to Mather, its fullest and finest expression in the work of Thomas Eakins and Winslow Homer. Homer, by far the greatest of the painter-reporters, and Eakins, most completely realistic of our painter-scientists, are now coming into a flood tide of popularity on the wave of artistic nationalism. Homer's *Prisoners from the Front* (Page 24) and *The Gulf Stream* (Page 24) present at their best the two main phases of his art. Eakins' *Max Schmitt in a Single Scull* (Page 22) reveals the artist's faithful attention to realistic detail and his scientific knowledge of anatomy.

Contrasting with the objective reality of Homer and Eakins is the imaginary world of the painter-poet Albert Pinkham Ryder, whose *Death on a Pale Horse* (Page 22) marks one of the high points in our earlier native expression. John Singer Sargent's *Wyndham Sisters* (Page 41) represents this successful internationalist at the height (or bottom) of his career in fashionable portraiture. Whistler's famous *Little White Girl* (Page 23) is a fine, typical example from the delicate brush of this noted expatriate, whose art was neither English nor American—but a derivative of French taste and Japanese pattern. The historical section ends with that powerful, dynamic *Stag at Sharkey's* (Page 42) by George Wesley Bellows, who, despite the influence of Manet as taught by Robert Henri, is as American as a Sears Roebuck catalogue. With Bellows our gallery of reproductions opens into the Twentieth Century.

Our Colonial Limners

While it is not the purpose of this book to give a detailed history of painting in America—that has been excellently done in the past by such notable art historians as William Dunlap, Henry T. Tuckerman, Samuel Isham, Sadakichi Hartmann, Suzanne La Follette and Alan Burroughs—a careful effort will be made here to trace briefly the currents of influence that have flowed into the stream of American art now swelling into a true national expression.

Most historians start the story of American art with John Smibert, a grimly realistic Scot who was a fellow student in London of William Hogarth (father of the glorious school of English portraiture). Thus the first great English painter preceded America's beginning by a scant fifty years—a fact art writers seldom mention in stressing our youth. About a century after the Pilgrims first set foot at Plymouth, Smibert came to the Colonies (1728) and married a Boston lady of "considerable fortune." Since then America has seen the ebb and flow of one foreign influence after another, with now and then a lonely native spirit raising his brush.

But even before Smibert, thrifty Puritan Fathers and rich Southern planters were willing to spend a few extra shillings to have their likenesses painted by the primitive, often nameless, Colonial limners —particularly in New England, where piety and prudery could not quite subdue the very human weakness of vanity. To the early settlers, however, art was a minor matter before the more serious struggle for a livelihood; the art of painting consisted of the static tracing of a physical likeness with a technique primitively imitative of the Dutch realism that flooded all of northern Europe on the wave of Anthony Van Dyck's popularity—without, however, any of the Dutch Master's gracious style or suave finish. Toward the close of the Seventeenth Century, with the solution of the original religious and economic problems that led to colonization, these limners dropped the Dutch influence and began to find in the English portraitists who followed Sir Godfrey Kneller (1646-1723) a more satisfactory, more pretentious realism.

A few of these early painters, like Thomas Smith and John Watson (a Scot who settled in Perth Amboy, N. J. and augmented his studio revenue with a pawnshop), are known. But most of the best Seventeenth Century American portraits are by forgotten artists—among them the portraits of the Gibbs children, done in Boston in 1670, fifty-eight years before Smibert's arrival.

Speaking of these pictures, the director of the Museum of Modern Art says: "Painted five years after the death of Poussin [and one year after the death of Rembrandt], they seem retarded in style by over a century; yet, as works of art, they have a charming and archaic dignity. They are the primitives of American art."

Malcolm Vaughan, thoroughly versed authority on America's painting past, enumerates the principal elements of our early art as: overemphasis of linear design, puritanical sobriety of palette; sobriety of creative expression, only partly puritanical; humanness of appeal, closely related to informality of thought; eager love of naturalism and, if one may add the spiritual characteristic overarching them all, homespun strength. Vaughan, who sees in these early portraits something distinctly American, claims that the overemphasis of linear design "was not a transportation from Europe. It had existed abroad from time to time in various schools of painting, but in Eighteenth and early Nineteenth Century foreign painting it was not dominant. In America it dominated the art. It was, of course, not self-conscious, not deliberate. On the contrary, its force is that it was natural. Doubtless it sprang from insufficient tutoring—untutored artists usually stress design."

Because of the very characteristics listed by Vaughan, sophisticated art lovers of today are showing increased interest in these rigid Colonial physiognomies, petrified in their Puritan dogma and shrewd self-sufficiency. It is the same kind of appreciation that is being showered on the loosely defined "popular" artists—unschooled, sincere craftsmen and amateurs who crudely painted neighborhood portraits, decorated signboards, carved figureheads for ships, cigar-store Indians, weather vanes, applied water color to velvet or glass, and produced other examples of American folk art now credited with an aesthetic value far out of proportion to their modest intentions.

Most distinguished of the "popular" artists were Edward Hicks, Quaker preacher and coach painter; Joseph Pickett, New Hope, Pennsylvania, carpenter and boatbuilder; and the more recent John Kane, Pittsburgh railroad worker who (like John Smibert and Adolf Hitler) began his art career as a house painter. Today's "Rousseau" may very well be canny Louis Eilshemius, whose flamboyant letters to the editors of New York newspapers in his old age first drew attention to the fact that he had painted 10,000 pictures, who has since sold three canvases to the Metropolitan Museum and has the unusual distinction of having three art dealers competing to become his agent—all this after three decades of neglect.

Copley and West

Aesthetically, American art begins with John Singleton Copley (1738-1815), who at the age of fifteen was able to paint a portrait of a Colonial preacher far finer than anything produced by such elder contemporaries as Joseph Badger. Badger's stiff, stylized, little men and women are as artificial as china dolls compared with even the earliest of Copleys. Even Joseph Blackburn, a fairly competent Scottish painter who came to Boston in 1755, was able to improve his art after studying the graceful posing, the softened outlines, the deeper modeling and the more assured drawing of Copley—thus reversing the traditional role of teacher and pupil.

By the time of Copley the Colonists had been settled for more than two generations, and a maturing culture had developed around a prosperous middle class in the North and around a wealthy landed gentry in the South, assuring a strong demand for the fine craftwork that we call American antiques today. The wilderness along the Eastern seaboard had been conquered; and there was time for leisure. Copley, who personified these more refined aspects of pre-Revolutionary culture, dominated New England painting until 1774 when, on the eve of the Revolution, he banished himself from American reality and settled in London. "Without imagination," records Alan Burroughs, "his taste for embellishment and grandiose effects naturally turned sour. He became the most stilted painter in England. However, in spite of his determination to be an Englishman, he had been one of the most skillful of self-taught American realists." Thus the son-in-law of the Boston Tory to whom was consigned the tea that made the Boston Tea Party blasted the first seed from which might have flowered an American art. "He knew more than all of us put together," lamented Gilbert Stuart. Charles C. Cunningham claims that only in our times has Copley recovered from the classification of an heirloom.

Benjamin West (1738-1820), born the same year as Copley and dying, like his New England contemporary, in London at an advanced age just as his vogue was starting to decline, was one of the finest, most generous characters in American art. Though he knew little of his native land, West had a profound influence on our early artists, teaching the English tradition to two generations of younger men who beat a path to the door of his London studio—among them Charles Willson Peale, Robert Fulton, Ralph Earl, John Trumbull, Samuel F. B. Morse, Gilbert Stuart, Washington Allston, Rembrandt Peale (son of C.W.) and Thomas Sully.

West arrived in London in 1763 at the age of twenty-five (after three years studying the old masters in Rome) and there knew the golden age that lives in the pages of James Boswell. Samuel Johnson was at the height of his wit and reputation, Reynolds was in the full tide of his success, Gainsborough and Wilson were producing their best paintings, Garrick was the darling of the stage and the mighty Hogarth had one more year of life. It was the dawn of the one great epoch in British painting. West painted in the grand manner the stories of history, of antique heroism and of biblical truth, and was saluted as a great artist. The King was his friend, he became president of the Royal Academy, and his social success encouraged many young Americans to try art as a profession. In 1801, when George III was in the last stages of insanity, West took advantage of the Peace of Amiens to visit Paris to see in the Louvre the vast collection of art Napoleon had plundered from all Europe, and was received with extreme honor by French artists and statesmen. But West was "Europe's worst daub, poor England's best," according to his contemporary, Byron, and modern scholars are inclined to agree. If his art was cold, formal and addicted more to the grand manner than to realities, West's Quaker character was a Gibraltar of kindness. He welcomed Copley, though Copley loomed as a rival. Samuel Johnson, who appears to have disapproved of West's art, was given a royal annuity through the artist's word to the King. He was buried with elaborate ceremonies in St. Paul's near Reynolds and Christopher Wren, as befitted a great English painter.

The Pupils of West

Charles Willson Peale (1741-1827), born three years after Copley and West, was, unlike his two famous contemporaries, an ardent patriot. He was in London studying with West in 1768 when Parliament annulled the New York Charter. Vowing never to "bend knee to an English King," he returned to Philadelphia, there to work out his destiny as a portrait painter of Revolutionary heroes and to found an artist-dynasty that kept the Peale name active for several generations (Rembrandt, Raphaelle, Rubens and Titian Peale were among his several sons). A man similar in public spirit to his fellow townsman, Benjamin Franklin, Peale was instrumental in organizing the Pennsylvania Academy of the Fine Arts in 1805. He also founded a museum of natural history in Philadelphia and, having a scientific bent—like such other early American painters as Audubon, Morse and Fulton— he made himself a set of porcelain false teeth when loss of his own interfered with his oratory.

John Trumbull (1756-1843), artist, soldier, politician, is remembered chiefly for his huge battle scenes and his portraits of Washington, Hamilton and other Revolutionary leaders. He exchanged his life's work with Yale University for an annuity. Matthew Pratt (1734-1805) is best known for the famous painting in the Metropolitan Museum showing the interior of West's studio. William Dunlap (1766-1839) is known as the "American Vasari"; his gossipy *History of the Arts of Design in the United States* is the foundation for early American art history. Two of West's most promising students, Robert Fulton (1765-1815) and Samuel F. B. Morse (1791-1872), were forced by lack of appreciation to turn from art to mechanical invention, the former to perfecting the steamboat and the latter to inventing the telegraph (after he had helped found the National Academy in 1826 and served as its first president). Morse's picture of the aged Lafayette, done during the famous Frenchman's farewell visit to America in 1825, belongs to the end of the Anglo-American tradition. Washington Allston (1779-1843), of the second generation of West's students, personified the popular drift away from the English tradition to the Italian. He painted in the grand Romantic style, recalling Salvator Rosa, Seventeenth Century Italian painter.

John Vanderlyn (1776-1852), who preferred Paris and Rome to London, came within a hair's breadth of making Americans appreciate the nude in art—and thereby advancing artistic progress at least two generations. "Vanderlyn," says Alan Burroughs, "almost succeeded in making the nude respectable at a time when husbands left the room when their wives changed stockings." Vanderlyn died in absolute want, but today his fame is on the rise. His most famous paintings are *Marius Sitting on the Ruins of Carthage*, painted in Rome in the style of David, founder of the Nineteenth Century French Classical school of painting; and his reclining nude, *Ariadne*, painted in Paris in 1812 and now housed in the Pennsylvania Academy of the Fine Arts. Sadikichi Hartmann ranks *Ariadne* as "the best nude this country has ever produced," though it was branded at the time by an American writer as "offending alike against pure taste and the morality of the art." Such an attitude on the part of their contemporary laymen makes it difficult to understand how early Americans painted as well as they did, or ever returned to brave the intolerant minds of their native land.

By far the greatest of West's students was Gilbert Stuart (1755-1828), son of a Scottish snuff grinder and of all our early artists the one who came closest to "painting American." Though he was exposed in London to the full force of England's golden age of portraiture—Raeburn, Reynolds and Gainsborough—he evolved an individual style, painting with a quick and sensitive touch, a silvery tonality of flesh and a shrewd eye for character. He avoided much of the flattery and elegant embellishments of his English colleagues. Unlike West and Trumbull, Stuart was faithful to his talent, ignoring grandiose effects and becoming the foremost portrait painter of his age.

After a highly successful career in England and Ireland, Stuart returned to America in 1792, impoverished by extravagant living, to take advantage of the new republic's insatiable demand for portraits of Washington. Stuart did three from life—the Vaughan, the Lansdowne and the Athenaeum —and, according to Mantle Fielding, painted one hundred and twenty-one variations from the three originals. His entire production is said to total more than 1,000 portraits. Justly styled the "valedictorian" of the English style in America and the most famous artist of the Federalist Period—within the formal end of the Revolution and the rise of Jeffersonian Democracy—Stuart was unable to transmit his technique to any successor. Nor was he able to establish a "school," unless we include his daughter, Jane Stuart, and the various copyists in such a category.

Stuart died in 1828 and was succeeded as the most popular portrait painter in America by Thomas Sully, whose chief influence was England's Sir Thomas Lawrence. Sully's son-in-law, John Neagle, indicated a coming trend in American art when in his best work, *Pat Lyon at the Forge*, he stressed the anecdotal element which was to flower in the next few decades. Today this element of storytelling, either prosaic or dramatic, is present in many of our finest canvases, as may be seen by *Janitor's Holiday* by Sample (Page 75) or *The Country Doctor* by Lauren Ford (Page 78).

The twilight of the long-dominating portrait painter was at hand. Seven years before the National Academy voted a fund to take care of the family of the dying Henry Inman, Morse, as president of the Academy, had given a speech in 1839 introducing to America a new mechanical invention, the camera. The introduction of the camera sounded the knell of the age-old function of the artist—to record facts as realistically as he was technically able. It sent him out on a search to find a more aesthetic, less mechanical, reason for being, to dredge other channels of economic security and to arrive eventually at the lifeless, ultra-aesthetic bones of nonobjective painting.

When Asher B. Durand gave up portraiture about 1839 to paint "a sort of dramatic scene in which a particular tree or aspect of nature may be called the principal figure," his move was in tune with his time. Artists, especially Thomas Doughty and Thomas Cole, were finding accurate paintings of nature the most popular form of art. Man no longer was solely interested in man, but, having subdued nature, was even willing to pay artists to paint aspects of natural beauty—providing they painted in the tight, realistic manner of the Düsseldorf Masters or the grand manner of French and Italian Romanticists.

An exciting period saw the first blooming of American landscape painting. By now the young United States had fought and won two wars with England, and was breeding around the question of slavery the most tragic war in our entire history. Progress in the United States was more rapid than in any European nation; canals and wagon routes had been greatly multiplied; there were 3,000 miles of railroads; population had almost tripled since the beginning of the century; the entire rich Mississippi Valley had been opened to settlement. Texas had been wrested from an impotent Mexico and the Alamo had become a symbol of the American spirit. Jacksonian Democracy, pledged to a "New Deal" for the new states against the bankers of the East, had emerged as "a people's victory" in 1828, and Old Hickory had put into words that basic principle of American politics: "To the victor belong the spoils." During the nation's first great financial depression that greeted the administration of Van Buren, Jackson's successor, progress continued under its own momentum.

In England the great Queen Victoria had ascended the throne, and Sir Thomas Lawrence, the last of Britain's brilliant portrait painters, had died. In France the dominant French middle class had come into power with Louis Philippe; the romanticists, Delacroix and Delaroche, had displaced the cold classicism of Napoleon's art dictator, David, and the Barbizon painter, Daubigny, was beginning to enjoy governmental patronage. It was a golden age of literature. In England there was active the brilliant galaxy of Browning, Dickens, Carlyle, Tennyson, Wordsworth, Macaulay, Southey and Thackeray. Balzac, Dumas and Gautier were writing in France. In America a new writer, Poe, had arisen to dispute the field with Longfellow and Whittier; Hawthorne had just published *Twice Told Tales*; and Emerson had begun the career that was to establish him as the foremost of our philosophic writers. Washington Irving was respected on both sides of the Atlantic; Cooper was ennobling the Red Man. American immigration was still from the north of Europe and our artistic temperament continued coldly literal, rather than emotional, resulting in the accomplished but usually uninspired paintings of the so-called "Hudson River School."

The Hudson River School

As applied to our early landscape painters the label, Hudson River School, is pretty much a misnomer. While the romantic Cole, co-founder of the school with the realistic Durand, started the tradition in the Catskills, it was not long before their followers deserted the boundless views of the Hudson River Valley. Bierstadt found his most faithful model in the mighty Rockies; Church was thrilled by the grandeur of the South American Andes; the fame of Thomas Moran, a later disciple, hangs on his views of the Yellowstone; and when Kensett, Gifford and Whittredge accompanied the expedition of General Pope to the Far West, the "Hudson River School" became indeed the "Rocky Mountain School."

Seldom has any group of artists enjoyed the monetary success of these landscapists. Americans showed their inherent love for a literary art by the demand they made for these canvases. Durand, when age had weakened his hand, was able to enjoy old age in peaceful, unworried retirement; Kensett became wealthy, and after his death in 1873 the paintings remaining in his studio sold at auction for $150,000; Bierstadt and Church brought prices that are the envy of contemporary landscape painters—$9,000 for a Church waterfall. The low prices they now bring at auction argue not against their literary content, but against their large size, monotonous detail and dry, thin color. The high prices in those days, however, went to artists who followed Europe most closely. Inness had little patronage until he absorbed the French Barbizons.

Durand during his long life of ninety years saw the landscape school born, flourish, fall from fashion; saw a new taste for foreign work (Hunt, La Farge, Whistler) arise, saw the young men desert Italy and Düsseldorf for the new gods of Paris and Munich. Church won the unique distinction of praise from the English critic, Ruskin, who was then widely read but little understood by Americans. Ruskin previously had condemned America: "I have just been seeing a number of landscapes by an American painter of some repute [Kensett]; and the ugliness of them is Wonderful. I see that they are true studies and that the ugliness of the country must be Unfathomable."

Bierstadt's huge panoramic canvases fetched as much as $15,000—extremely high prices when compared with the bids on landscape work today. To explain the size of Kensett's canvases, Alan Burroughs quotes a critic of 1853 who wrote: "The future spirit of our art must be inherently vast like our western plains, majestic like our forests, generous like our rivers." That, of course, was before Americans started to live in kitchenette-and-bath apartments. Living artists, like Lucioni and Klitgaard, measure their landscapes in inches not feet.

Inness and His Followers

About 1860 the fame of the Barbizon School in France had spread to America and under its influence—which lasted until the importation of Monet's impressionism—the somber, dry color of the Hudson Riverists took on new depth, fresh vitality and our landscapes assumed greater aesthetic value through a new harmony of line and mass. The early Hudson Riverists were followed by George Inness, Alexander Wyant and Homer D. Martin. Of the three George Inness (1825-1894) was easily the greatest.

Though in his second period an ardent admirer of Corot, Inness, like Stuart, approached close to the American spirit. His skill in rendering light with brilliancy and his mastery of atmospheric tonality were bound up strongly with his love of the American Scene, the abundance and fertile beauty of his native land. As in *Peace and Plenty* (Pages 20-21), Inness was most attracted by expansive, idyllic scenes and the calmer moments of nature which he delighted in idealizing with luminous light. Inness, whose career covers the transitional period between the precise German painting of Durand and the romantic conceptions of the French landscapists, believed that the landscape belonged in the realm of emotion, not fact, and succeeded in penetrating beneath a photographic fidelity. "The purpose of the painter," said Inness, "is simply to reproduce in other minds the impression which a scene has made upon him. A work of art does not appeal to the intellect. It does not appeal to the moral sense. Its aim is not to instruct, not to edify, but to awaken an emotion." Therein Inness was akin to some of the moderns.

Inness' late manner was emulated with uneven success by his followers. The theory of transcribing intimate emotions drew to a doubtful conclusion in the French-inspired landscapes of J. Francis Murphy, who achieved wide success with his sentimentalized views. The greatest follower of Inness was Ralph Blakelock (1847-1919), whose peculiarly lighted moonlit canvases seem shadowed with the tragic melancholy that was to end in his insanity. Blakelock, like Ryder, was a poet of paint, though a minor poet, and one of our most individual artists.

Homer D. Martin (1836-1897) was much older than his fellows when he first went abroad, and consequently was influenced by a different type of landscape—the high-keyed, French impressionistic paintings of Monet, Sisley and Pissarro. Martin, seeking to remedy his lack of power, adopted a little of the impressionistic technique: his greatest picture, *Harp of the Winds* in the Metropolitan Museum, is almost a study in illumination. Martin was the last of the important exponents of landscape in the American manner before the Civil War. After him came the thoroughly impressionist painters, most of whom retained much of their American realism and obtained more solidity of form than did their idol, Monet.

Chief among these American landscape impressionists are: John W. Twachtman, who discarded his earlier Munich-acquired brown shadows to paint with broken, sparkling light; J. Alden Weir, who switched from the realism of Manet to the impressionism of Monet, yet obtained considerable strength of form; Theodore Robinson, close friend of Monet, who insisted on strong draftsmanship; Maurice Prendergast, one of the very few great artists New England has produced since Homer, whose tapestry-like patterns had felt the stimulation of modern expressionism; and Childe Hassam, perhaps the finest of the American impressionists, who kept his spirited individuality as he painted the mood of light on objects of solidity and weight.

The impressionist technique, founded on a scientific theory—the refracted rays of the spectrum on objects in sunlight—and one of the very few original ideas in art since the Italians solved perspective and Van Eyck perfected the oil medium, has retained its popularity into the present era. Impressionism was viciously fought by the followers of Bouguereau—painter of those prim, neo-classic maidens who are now sometimes called "barroom nudes." Today it is an accepted, academic method of painting, a dominant influence in the work of the president of the National Academy, Jonas Lie.

However, a tour of any national exhibition will show that most of the practitioners of impressionism are artists over thirty-five. The art student, conscious of the tide of nationalism around him, fears being caught with a French technique, much as he avoids the surface imitation of Cézanne, so prevalent between 1926 and 1930. During those years students in most parts of the country were exposed to third- and fourth-rate Cézannes, which in many cases were in an unfinished state, thinly scrubbed and ofttimes with plenty of canvas showing. Here was a short-cut away from the hard work of learning their craft, and the students were quick to imitate the failures of the master. The result was the appearance in national exhibitions of many thirty-second cousins of Cézanne, all decked out in rainbow color.

Indicative of the change are the instructions which the Pennsylvania Academy stresses in awarding its annual Cresson scholarships. Much is made of the fact that students who are leaving the Academy have completed a thorough American academic training, and that the scholarships are not intended to be used for art study abroad. Rather, as the officials outline it, the students are to take advantage of the important museums and cultural atmosphere which the Old World has to offer, but are urged to continue their experiments in America where native environment will give them a more natural development.

Genre Painters

America, since the Revolution, has produced a long line of genre painters who delighted in everyday scenes, artists stemming generally from English or German literalness who painted the story of America "for the common man." Throughout the pages of our art history are scores of these artists—good, bad or indifferent—who with little conscious aesthetics worked in an idiom that spoke directly to every American layman, such artists as Blythe, Bingham, Mount, Johnson, Colman, Quidor and the sentimental Hovenden. In the days before the camera and before photoengraving, they were the pictorial troubadours of the people. Today they are being reexamined in the colder light of higher aesthetics and more than one is finding new appreciation.

These genre works meet on a common ground of style and purpose, and the challenge is there to the modern eye to select those which speak in terms of great art from those which lack genius. This type of painting, which the connoisseur of a few years ago dismissed with scorn, is now coming into favor—possibly as a by-product of the wave of nationalism that sent us back to examine anew our origins and our native traditions. Without doubt there is a growing movement, a resurgent appreciation in American art values that will free to the light of day a goodly number of paintings which have been in hiding during the blustering, swaggering days of aesthetic esotericism—interned in the morgue we have so conveniently labeled "sentimentality."

During the process of rediscovery much attention has been paid to William Sidney Mount, David G. Blythe, George Bingham, Eastman Johnson and William Harnett.

About the time the grandiose visions of Allston and Trumbull were going into eclipse, William S. Mount, self-taught son of a Long Island farmer, entered art after a humble apprenticeship as a sign painter. Sometimes called the "Jan Steen of Long Island," Mount knew, loved and understood the life he painted with such natural feeling—farmers, field hands, tavernkeepers, dancing, fighting, drinking, working. His was a rural Long Island before real-estate operators carved out their developments and businessmen organized the great World's Fair on Flushing Dump.

Important among the earlier American Scene painters was George Caleb Bingham (1811-1879), who grew up along the Mississippi in the "Mark Twain" country and was a homespun product of frontier life and Düsseldorf training. Bingham has been classified by Alfred H. Barr, Jr., director of the Museum of Modern Art—New York citadel of sophisticated art—as one of the "best American artists of the mid-century. He was completely and happily a man of his time and place, an influential citizen, a public figure who on one occasion won a political election through the eloquence of his painted propaganda. But the obvious illustrative interest of his art rested upon an instinctive gift for composition and a sound, if somewhat literal, technique." Bingham was the nation's best pictorial reporter during the decades immediately following the main Trans-Appalachian "push," just as Winslow Homer—the greatest of our painter-reporters—was during the Civil War period and the Reconstruction Era.

David G. Blythe (1815-1865), an itinerant wood carver and portrait painter who settled in Pittsburgh in the mid-century and turned a satirical yet twinkling eye on his fellows, has gained a growing army of admirers today. Alan Burroughs, who claims Blythe painted roisterously in the combined style of Ostade and Brouwer, turning cherubs into sneak thieves and noble citizens into sly carpetbaggers, writes: "If it is strange that little has been made till recently of the work of Bingham, and nothing of the work of Mount, it is stranger still that Blythe has remained unknown outside of Pittsburgh."

Eastman Johnson (1824-1906), who painted common subjects with a natural sincerity and aesthetic feeling, has, on the other hand, never lacked admirers. Returning to America in 1860 after working with Leutze in Düsseldorf, Johnson painted numerous anecdotal canvases—like *Old Kentucky Home* (Page 19) and *Husking Bee*—which appealed to the people not alone for their popular subject matter but also for their aesthetic qualities. Today John McCrady, down in New Orleans, has likewise found inspiration in America's folk ballads (see *Swing Low, Sweet Chariot,* Page 99).

Contemporary with Mount, Blythe and Bingham, though working in a different category, were John James Audubon (1785-1851) and George Catlin (1796-1872), two of America's greatest painter-scientists. Audubon, celebrated ornithologist, student of David in Paris and once suspected of being the famous Lost Dauphin, was completing his magnificent series of paintings of the Birds of America; and Catlin was painting the noble and yet un-Cooperish portraits of Indians now in the United States National Museum. Audubon, even during the long Hoover-Roosevelt depression, has been breaking auction records; and Catlin, who sometimes achieved effects as fine as the Nineteenth Century Frenchman Constantine Guys, is sure to enjoy wider appreciation during the coming years.

The Expatriates

The last third of the last century saw American art enter upon its greatest period of artistic ventriloquism, a period of vast material growth but one of widespread atrophy of the national art spirit —probably the lowest point of our almost continuous echoing of European painting. This was the age in which the expatriates Whistler, Sargent and Cassatt were proclaimed our finest painters. Left standing like a lonely rock in swirling seas of foreign art fashions was the great triumvirate of native American artists, Homer, Ryder and Eakins.

These were the decades of America's young manhood—some term it "robust vulgarity"—the formative years as we developed into a world power of 75,000,000 people. The four tragic years of the Civil War had bled the United States white. But so strong was the national vitality that the march of progress paused only momentarily. The martyred Lincoln was followed by the friendless Johnson; Grant, who had too many friends, succeeded Johnson and raised the "third term" question for the second time; Cyrus Field further shortened the distance between two points with the first transatlantic cable; Alaska was purchased from Russia, and at Ogden, Utah, the continent was physically linked by bands of steel. "Black Friday" in 1869, when Vanderbilt, Gould and Fisk tried to corner the gold, foretold the coming of S.E.C. to control our legal crooks. The difference between the Tweed scandal of 1873 and several of our present-day city administrations is that we have no Thomas Nast to say quietly, "Let Us Prey."

When Lee died five years after the surrender at Appomattox, exploitation of our natural resources was gathering impetus. Great fortunes were being made in railroads, lumber, cattle, land, coal, oil and gold; newly rich Americans were building some of the ugliest houses man has ever seen (so ugly, in fact, that modern artists try to paint the beauty of their souls). In those ugly houses were installed the artistic monstrosities of the Victorian Age, and art dealers first began the wholesale importation of foreign art—Barbizons, pretty little genre pictures, and the reigning salonniers, Bouguereau, Gerome and Meissonier. Mark Twain was writing a book called *Innocents Abroad*, not thinking, perhaps, how aptly his title applied to the hundreds and hundreds who crowded the ateliers of Paris and Munich.

Today American art schools are thoroughly equipped to give the young American the best training obtainable; but in 1900, and for almost twenty-five years after, art instruction was plainly stamped "Made in France." During that stretch of almost seventy years the position of Paris as the font of foreign influence was challenged but once, by Chase and Duveneck, who took their pupils to Munich in the 1870s.

The Ecole des Beaux Arts and the Academies of Julian and Colarossi attracted hundreds of young Americans, some serious students, others charmed by Bohemian liberty and intent on sowing a few wild oats. Gerome taught Thayer, Weir, Eakins and Bridgman; Lefebvre taught Dewing and Vonnoh; Carolus-Duran had as students Sargent, Low and Beckwith. Bouguereau and Bonnat were other popular teachers, with wide American followings.

Several justly famous artists emerged during this later period of foreign domination, but what today's advocates of an American School object to is that they were not Americans in the national sense of the term. They had lost touch with their native heath, had lost that intangible ingredient we call the American spirit. William Morris Hunt brought the refined taste of the wealthy, intellectual cosmopolitan back to America. Never much more than an aristocratic amateur, he said at the end of his career: "In another country, I might have been a painter." John La Farge, friend of Hunt, was America's first great ecclesiastical artist, notable for his work in stained glass and his murals in Trinity Church, Boston, and the Church of the Ascension and St. Thomas' in New York. La Farge's characteristic refinement of artistic perception is most evident in his neglected landscapes. His sons and grandsons have made the name La Farge live in the realm of art and letters.

Three famous American artists of this era—James MacNeill Whistler, John Singer Sargent and Mary Cassatt—chose to stay in Europe rather than brave the unpolished taste of their rough and turbulent homeland. They commanded eloquent brushes but they spoke in glittering generalities that contained little of lasting significance for the generations of Americans to follow.

Whistler, greatest of these expatriates, fine painter but finer etcher, blended within the strong individuality of his sensitive nature the refined aesthetics of the French and the delicate patterns of Japanese art. He loved London, a contrary mistress who preferred the caresses of Ruskin and the "philistines." In English eyes he committed heresy when he stressed color, not subject. "Whistler," notes clear-thinking Dorothy Grafly of the Philadelphia *Record* in her invaluable articles on the *Parade of American Art,* "dared break with what England considered art. He even dared, before the advent of the impressionists, to steal their thunder. By placing emphasis on color patterns, he paved the way for abstraction." England, France, America, each can be proud of Whistler, true internationalist; none can claim him. The aestheticism of the Whistlerian butterfly retains but a minor role in the forthright art of today's America.

Europeans can also understand and appreciate Sargent, most lionized international portrait painter of his generation. Sargent's fashionable portraits, at their lowest level, bear a family resemblance to the work of contemporary foreign portrait painters who obtain rich American commissions with the assistance of artistically illiterate society leaders and some of our francophile society magazines. Sargent, gifted with a naturally fluent brush and a brilliancy of technique that was further sharpened in the atelier of Carolus-Duran, enjoyed a popular success that was equaled only by Velasquez, Rubens and Van Dyck. After his death in London in 1925, his paintings and sketches went under the auctioneer's hammer at Christie's and fetched $850,000—an enduring record. In 1929 his huge *Wyndham Sisters (The Three Graces)* (Page 41) was purchased by the Metropolitan Museum with 90,000 Wolfe dollars, an extraordinary price that probably would be cruelly decimated at auction today. Where idolatry once went beyond reason, devaluation has now gone too far, as modern critics remember too well the commercial shallowness of such portraits as the Metropolitan Museum's *Mrs. Stokes.* An exhibition of Sargent's noncommercial, nonfashionable works would render an excellent service to the artist's memory.

To the French, Mary Cassatt is the greatest American woman painter—her taste was their taste; her art, particularly those exquisite Mother and Child themes with which she so often indulged the yearnings of a starved nature, was entirely of their tradition. The French understand Mary Cassatt, who knew nothing of American art. Daughter of a wealthy Philadelphia banker, friend of Degas, Miss Cassatt fought passionately for the impressionist rebels, practically built the Havemeyer Collection of impressionistic paintings and gave the market for French art in America tremendous encouragement. Dorothy Grafly recounts that "when one of the great French dealers [Durand-Ruel] was about to go bankrupt because he had invested too heavily in work that had not yet found a market, she came to his rescue financially, and with brilliant business acumen, through American collectors, who were her friends, and American dealers, who were theirs, opened up in the United States an enthusiasm for French art that still dominates the market."

Miss Grafly gives a vivid account of the concluding chapter in the life of America's last great expatriate, before the end came in 1927 in her chateau at Mesnil-Beaufresne: "Blindness was closing in on her. Ruthlessly she had pushed nature aside for the demands of her art. Now it retaliated. She was a stranger in a strange land. Long ago she had lost contact with the America that now, so pathetically, became her last passion, when she was no longer part of it. In Paris, American students were wasting their time in superficialities. She would wave her stick toward the left bank in a gust of anger bolstered by profanity. 'Café loafers,' she called them. Expatriotism, she declared, was destroying them. 'When I was young it was different,' she said. 'Our Museums had no great paintings for the students to study. That has been corrected and something must be done to save our young American artists from wasting themselves.'"

Munich in the 1870s competed with Paris as the source of foreign art education. Today the link between Munich teachers—notably Duveneck and Chase—and the art of our times remains closer than that with Paris. This is undoubtedly because Munich, like the moderns, placed the accent on strength and vitality of technique, broad planes and spontaneous execution. Frank Duveneck, great teacher for a quarter-century in Cincinnati, was the very essence of the Munich tradition, going back to Frans Hals for his robust vigor, his broadly brushed forms and his strong contrasts of dark and light. With spontaneous vitality he delighted in his strength, and was always, whether in Cincinnati, Boston or Munich, an inspiring and generous leader among his fellows. Since his death in 1919, his art—despite the defect of dark bituminous backgrounds—has held its own.

Of all the Munich men, the one who exerted the greatest influence upon American painting was William M. Chase, a versatile genius who insisted on technique ahead of subject matter—he preached that there is paintable beauty in a dead fish, and he and his famous follower, Charles W. Hawthorne, proved it in many a canvas. Some of our present-day artists have carried the Chase theory to its ultimate conclusion and waited for the fish to decompose. Chase topped his Courbet-Hals training in Munich with a dash of Velasquez—the source of Manet's strong realism, which in turn proved the inspiration for the American realists after the turn of the century. Of all the foreign influences that have touched American art, Manet's has been the most lasting in the light of present-day events. Chase, charming yet assertive advocate of technique and craftsmanship, was another of America's great painter-teachers, and has through his many still active students become a strong tie between the art of the past and the present. Chase many times remarked during his criticisms at the Pennsylvania Academy: "Chain an artist to his doorstep and he will find himself surrounded by the beauty of the world."

The position of Chase in relation to our contemporary painting is well stated by Alan Burroughs: "Among his pupils were the men who were to carry vitality of technique deep into American art and to practice the principle stated so simply by Eakins, that 'if America is to produce great painters and if young art students wish to assume a place in the history of the art of their country, their first desire should be to remain in America, to peer deeper into the heart of American life.'"

America's Native Triumvirate

Homer. Ryder. Eakins. These are America's old masters, the star witnesses we place on the stand when older nations accuse us of being too young or too heterogeneous to produce an art of our own. These three artists were generally misunderstood by their contemporaries. About their easels the fashionable influences of European painting fell unheeded. Though their characters and their art had little in common, they were brothers in more than one respect: each followed his destiny on American soil; each visited Europe but returned untouched by fashionable European superficialities; each retained this artistic independence in an age when Europe was the arbitrator of American painting; and each refused to compromise with a society that would not accord him recognition.

Homer said, "When I have selected the thing carefully I paint it exactly as it appears." In both the selection and in the painting he was guided by an inherent, instinctive sense of design and color. He gave the external world of fact an internal soul of Pure Art—a process similar to the present development of our American Scene painters—men like Gifford Beal and Andrew Wyeth. Ryder, with no Old World tradition to guide his untrained brush, sought refuge from his times in the poetic visions of his own imaginative world, a world that no American has ever seen but one that only a romantic American has ever dreamed. Some of his mystic feeling is caught today by Henry Mattson.

Eakins, like Homer, lived in an objective world and his patron saint was Truth. And because of his artistic integrity and his power of three-dimensional feeling he penetrated well below the surface of factual appearances. To have your portrait painted by Eakins was to be psychoanalyzed in public. Homer, Ryder, Eakins, each peered "deeper into the heart of American life," whether objective or imaginative.

To young Americans of today the healthy, objective worlds of Homer and Eakins are more important than the sophisticated, decorative output of Picasso, Matisse or Dufy—so today our exhibitions contain fewer little Picassos, fewer little Matisses, and the French say we have no native art.

Ryder, too, has a peculiarly contemporary meaning. Says Alfred H. Barr, Jr.: "Ryder's dreams of clouded moonlight over troubled seas, of death and witches lurking in uncanny shadows are prophetic of a contemporary nostalgia for the romantic, the mysterious and the sentimental which gains strength daily"—namely the surrealists, "artists intent upon realizing spontaneous images capable of evoking sentiment."

The realistic strain in the American nature found its fullest expression in the art of Winslow Homer, a born draftsman of tremendous power, who, hardened by years of Civil War illustrations, sensed the larger contours of nature and applied his color with the canny hand of a great and dramatic artist. Largely self-taught—he had only slight formal training at the National Academy—Homer became our greatest painter-reporter of the Civil War era and later our greatest marine painter. Visits to Europe in his mature years did not alter one iota his forthright American Yankee spirit.

Has there ever been a true American Old Master? The question is answered in complete affirmative by Winslow Homer. With all the once damning qualities of realism, illustrative quality, lack of a conscious aesthetics, reverence for the seen fact and humility before nature, Homer emerges a master of the tradition that is the American naissance of today. Study a Homer painting and you will understand America.

When Homer summed up his aesthetics for a friend with the statement that he first carefully selected a subject and then painted it exactly as it appeared, that statement was no reflection on the aesthetics of his art. Like the hardy Yankee he was, with forebears who wrenched a living from the most refractory soil in America, Homer made nature work for him. He selected carefully and in his careful selection was instinctive design; the canvas was half done before it was started. He was objective, respectful and reserved as he handled nature. A form was never tortured; he painted what he saw, and, like some of our American Sceners of today, gave what he saw the essence of aesthetic truth.

Strength is an ever-recurring characteristic of American art. Homer's strength shows in his art and in his character. He made the usual grand tour of Europe, came back unaffected by salon art and continued to paint as a naturalist. When he was forty-five he went to England, there worked in water color and underwent his main change in style. He saw the larger aspects of nature, painted in more subtle tones and struck a deeper, more heroic, note in his sea dramas. And he remained, as may be seen by his last water color, *Shipwreck*, now owned by the St. Louis Art Museum, a strong-fibered American Yankee until the very end.

That other dominating strain that weaves constantly through American life, the imaginative, romantic, idealistic feeling that produced the poetry of Edgar Allan Poe and the ballads of Stephen Foster, had in painting a direct counterpart in Albert Pinkham Ryder, most individual of our artists, who lived with shadowy fantasies and moonlit visions. Ryder had no Old World tradition to guide him, no foreign technique to show him how to paint his poetry. His training, like Homer's, was negligible; his system was the old one of trial and error, as he worked and reworked to transmute pigment into the romantic dreaming that lies so close beneath the American's blunt and fatalistic exterior. Americans are essentially dreamers, sentimental and idealistic, and Ryder was the voice of depths seldom sounded in our art.

Twice in later life Ryder went abroad, but Europe's masters left little impression. His art was too individual, too closely locked within the soul and mind of this unkempt hermit, whom Barr terms "half saint, half bohemian." "The artist needs but a roof, a crust of bread and his easel, and all the rest God gives him in abundance," Ryder once said. Providence, through the agency of friends, must have also supplied the roof and the crust, for Ryder's art was too native to be appreciated in those days of transatlantic worship.

Bryson Burroughs, writing in the catalogue of the Modern Museum's great Homer-Ryder-Eakins exhibition, said: "Ryder's pictures show him to have been peculiarly susceptible to the eeriness of night, as children are, and to have had their happy faculty of fusing inextricably in their own minds imaginary and real experiences. In those night walks of his which we hear about, was it the streets and the factories, the tedious line of houses, that he saw, and the people of the pavement? I doubt it. He looked at palaces with pinnacles, I believe, and castles and towers; at enchanted princesses and the great ladies of Romance and lovely knights; at the Thane of Glamis as he met the Witches in Union Square; and at Melusine with a dulcimer at the window on Fourteenth Street. . . . He was a belated incarnation of the romantic spirit of the early Nineteenth Century."

Thomas Eakins, like his friend Walt Whitman, saw beauty in everything around him, and, though he got his training in France, his pictures, imbued with native dignity and unbridled masculine power, show him an artist distinctly American and uninfluenced by any foreign ancestry. Bryson Burroughs called him "the most consistent of American realists." Lloyd Goodrich in his Eakins biography draws a sharp distinction between Sargent's purely visual realism and Eakins' "intellectual realism." Eakins gave a new meaning to America's strain of realism. His vision was almost photographic in its keenness of observation; his mind had the analytical clarity of a scientist's; and it was through this combination of vision, mind and aesthetic feeling that he was able to catch the American character.

Eakins was greatest in his portraits, not from choice but from necessity. Eakins, who served as professor of anatomy in Philadelphia for several years, knew the construction of the human figure better than any other artist of his time, and he loved the nude. But after battling his narrow, prudish environment, the pagan side of his nature was forced to conform—much as Vanderlyn had been beaten down by the Sumners of seventy-five years before. Eakins fought and was later molded by that third American characteristic, the desire to mind other people's business, to legislate morals and to impose censorship. With all of our vaunted constitutional liberties, most of us have never learned that great humans demand one additional freedom—freedom of the spirit. Our contemporary artists must still battle this puritanical hangover.

The best summation of Eakins, third of our native triumvirate, was written by Lloyd Goodrich: "With all his limitations, Eakins was the strongest formal composer among the American painters of his generation, and one of the strongest anywhere. Others had a more pleasing gift of pattern and decoration, but few had his sculptured sense of form or his instinct for three-dimensional design. In this country only Ryder shared these qualities, having more sense of movement and rhythm and a more complete conception of the whole picture, while Eakins dealt with more powerful elements, and created forms of greater solidity and force on a more monumental scale." As in any Anglo-Saxon civilization, America favors a three-dimensional art, and it is this, together with his intellectual realism and sculptural form, that makes Eakins so close to us today—so American.

In the opinion of Edward Alden Jewell of the New York *Times,* Eakins "traversed all the hazards of academic instruction in Paris, retaining what was calculated to be of real value to him and emerging from the tutelage miraculously unvitiated by the meretricious style of Jean Leon Gerome." Jewell feels that Homer, Ryder and Eakins form a trio that "does much to solidify and ennoble our slowly unfolding American tradition. And it furnishes us with a sort of measure by means of which we may the more confidently appraise other artists of the same period or of succeeding decades."

Ryder left no followers. Eakins left a young army. Through Thomas Anschutz, his pupil and colleague at the Pennsylvania Academy, the essence of Eakins' philosophy and his art principles has passed down to the living generation, for Anschutz was the early teacher of those leaders of "The Eight," Henri, Sloan, Luks, Shinn and Glackens.

The Eight of 1908

As the new century dawned, The Eight brought American painting back from the roseate clouds of the Victorian Era, deposited it with a resounding thud of reality on American soil and anticipated by almost twenty-five years the American Scene nationalism of today. It was not the fault of these eight artists—Arthur B. Davies, William J. Glackens, Robert Henri, Ernest Lawson, George Luks, Maurice Prendergast, Everett Shinn and John Sloan—that they did not complete the crusade of freeing American painting from its three centuries of subservience to European fashion. They could not very well stop the World War or check the rising tide of French modernism. It should be remembered that The Eight held their First (and last) Annual Exhibition the year Cubism was born in Paris. Three—Sloan, Shinn and Lawson—are still living, and their veteran eyes undoubtedly gleam with satisfaction when they see the emancipation in the work of their post-war successors.

Then as now, nationalism was in the air. America, fresh from a victorious war with Spain, was embarking upon the course of imperial expansion that was later to see her assume the status of a world power. Industry was undergoing tremendous development; electricity and automobiles were becoming necessities; the first Roosevelt was wielding the big stick over the trusts; and wealth was increasing at an amazing rate. Immigration switched—and this is important in tracing our contemporary artists—from the north of Europe to the southern and eastern section, bringing in Italians, Spaniards, Hungarians, Roumanians, Bulgars, Slavs, Poles and Russians whose sons and daughters are mainly responsible for the warm blood that has now crept into American painting.

Periodically an event occurs in the art world that reverberates down through the years; such an

The Wyndham Sisters—JOHN SINGER SARGENT

Stag at Sharkey's—George Wesley Bellows

Sunday, Women Drying Their Hair—JOHN SLOAN

Wake of the Ferry No. 2—JOHN SLOAN

Flood Refugees—Jon Corbino

Over the Dam—Charles E. Burchfield

Six O'Clock—Charles E. Burchfield

Noon—Doris Lee

event was the revolutionary exhibition of The Eight at the old Macbeth Gallery in New York in 1908. The previous year had witnessed the absorption of the Society of American Artists (the young rebels of the late Nineteenth Century) by the venerable National Academy. The eight "men of rebellion" loomed suddenly on the artistic horizon as a new and vigorous opposition. They preached realism, but more particularly they insisted that art must spring from everyday life, be of the common man.

Henri, Luks, Glackens, Shinn and Sloan all came from Philadelphia where they had studied under Anschutz, heir to Eakins' realism. With the single exception of Henri, the unofficial leader, the Philadelphians had worked as illustrators on newspapers, and though Tolstoy, Whitman, Bellamy and Henry George may be cited as the source of their philosophy, the shouted orders of a city editor to "get the human interest angle" may have been a more direct influence.

The rebellion of The Eight was, in the main, against the currently popular academic pretty pictures, the pseudoclassical masquerades of grandeur, the "Venus in Cheesecloth" allegories and the slavish copies of Paris Salon favorites. William Dean Howells had advanced the precept that "the smiling aspects of life were the more American." This comfortable, insipid doctrine stood at the opposite pole to the sterner principles of The Eight, who were variously dubbed the "Ashcan School" and the "Revolutionary Black Gang." Stemming from the traditions of Manet and Velasquez, with a still lingering Munich and impressionist influence, their paintings were largely rebellious only to the extent of choosing unorthodox subject matter. But in those days of decorous virgins and salon portraits, it was rampant radicalism to dare to be a realist and paint the American Scene. "It isn't the subject that counts but what you feel about it," said Henri, and his colleagues dedicated themselves to the ideal that the artist must paint the life he knows best if he would be American.

Helen Appleton Read appropriately comments in the Whitney Museum's "New York Realists" catalogue that "a younger generation may recognize that many of the precepts by which they steer their course were charted by the group which rallied around Robert Henri in the decade before the War. For the Tolstoian precept that art should be a means of uniting men was expressed by Henri with his characteristic mingling of pithy simile and abstract idealism when he said: 'To have an art in America will not be to sit like a pack rat on a pile of collected art of the past. It will be rather to build our own projection on the art of the past, wherever it may be, and for this constructiveness, the artist, the man of means, and the man on the street should go hand in hand.'

"As time gives perspective to our judgments, it becomes increasingly evident that the moderns of the first Roosevelt era represented an historic chapter in American art, to which we owe a great debt. For not only did they prepare the way for the inquiring liberal spirit which made the modern movement an inevitable next step, but they implanted in our subconscious minds the belief that all significant art has its roots deep in the soil that produced the artist, and that we must link our present with our past. And they also sowed the seeds for that integration of art and society that has become so vital an issue today."

When one looks back it is difficult to realize that these artists were once regarded by the effete as iconoclastic radicals, vulgar vilifiers of the Vestal Virgin, Art. It was not their way of painting that earned The Eight their reputation as breakers of idols; it was their way of looking at life. They were as dissimilar in character and technique as our earlier native triumvirate; neither were they all realists in the accepted sense of the term.

Prendergast and Davies belonged to the group more because of their individualism than their painting. Both working in the lone, visionary bypaths of subject matter, they upheld and encouraged the right of every artist to be free, personal and himself. Davies, creator of such romantic visions as *I Hear America Singing*, was a sensitive eclectic in the line of La Farge, but also touched the realm of Ryderesque poetry. Prendergast, an impressionist who was probably the first American artist to appreciate the power of Cézanne, painted ethereal tapestrylike designs in soft, rich greens and blues. One of those rare artists who, through their intrinsic worth, win the plaudits of conservatives and liberals alike, Prendergast has a following today that is almost fanatical in its worship.

Lawson and Glackens were the outright impressionists of the group, the former painting lyrically more in the manner of Monet, and the latter turning, after a successful career in black and white, to the beautiful porcelain color of Renoir—greatest of the French impressionists and probably the greatest of all French painters. Lawson, still active with his "palette of crushed jewels," was the only one of The Eight to seek his inspiration predominantly in the open country.

The Philadelphians—Henri, Luks, Sloan and Shinn—were the four chiefly responsible for the group's classification as realist, with Luks and Sloan working hardest from the "ashcan" point of view. All of them utilized man as the main element in their art. But with them man suffered, laughed or worked, far differently from the idyllic figures that appear in most of Davies' paintings, which show cavorting children in a sunny expanse of forest, a group of nudes against a pastoral backdrop, virginal girlish forms garbed in diaphanous veils emerging from mist. Children laugh and dance in Luks' *The Spielers*, but it is the high-strung, transitory laughter of New York's slum children. No, it was not their way of painting that held The Eight together as potent forces for a true American art.

Sloan's views of Manhattan stand out for their lightning snatches of reality in Times Square, Sixth Avenue and the Bowery. His fame as an artist will hang heavily on his earlier periods before the Armory Show and particularly upon such pungent chronicles of New York life as *McSorley's Bar, Wake of the Ferry No. 2* (Page 44), *Sunday, Women Drying Their Hair* (Page 43). Henri, who reached his full stature of greatness only as a teacher, brought the tradition of Manet and Velasquez to bear on such subjects as *Fifty-seventh Street* and *Storm Tide* and *New York Street in Winter*. Where his reputation has been injured by his too numerous Spanish portraits, it has been made secure by his greatest painting, the *Portrait of George Luks* (done somewhat in Luks' lusty style). Shinn, admirer of Degas, blended realism with gaiety as he depicted theatrical life. His most famous painting is *London Music Hall*, owned by the Metropolitan Museum. Luks added the boisterous vitality of a Frans Hals to Manet's realism, mixed them thoroughly with his own American spirit, and painted American life with a zest that has never been equaled.

In this group of earlier American Scene painters should be included George Bellows, Glenn Coleman and Guy Pène du Bois, famous pupils of Henri, and also that lone eagle of American art, George "Pop" Hart, full-living world traveler, who laughed at life and caught that laughter on the tip of his brush or etching needle. A powerful, untrained draftsman, Hart was too much of an individualist to be one of even "eight." His was a great talent and a great soul.

Bellows, born of pioneer American stock and trained in Henri's art philosophy, was, according to Helen Appleton Read, "the apotheosis of the one hundred per cent American artist. In his early canvases there is evidenced not only his boundless zest for life and his unerring sense of the dramatic instant of life (to borrow a phrase from Eugene Speicher), but there is also an indication of that quality which characterized his later work—the ability to relate his material, however realistic or contemporary it might be, to some universal truth. His work also had definite social implications. Bellows believed that painting was not meant for the few but should be an interpretation of common experience possible of being shared by all. His belief in the social function of art is expressed in the following quotation:

" 'All civilization and culture are the results of the creative imagination or artist quality in man. The artist is the man who makes life more interesting or beautiful, more understandable or mysterious, or probably more beautiful in the best sense. His trade is to deal in illimitable experience.' "

Bellows painted the most tender and most deeply felt child portraits ever done in America. His greatest canvas is his portrait of Catherine Rosen; his most famous are *Edith Cavell* and *Stag at Sharkey's* (Page 42).

The Eight of 1908, now sadly depleted by time, left a cultural heritage that has been invaluable to our contemporary artists who have built a native American art by painting the life they live. They launched something that becomes increasingly comprehensible as the American spirit fires the brushes of our artists.

The Eight's adulation of Manet and Velasquez was one thing—in fact, a pretty common thing in American art history during the past seventy years. Their city-room camaraderie was something else. Working on Philadelphia newspapers covering murders, fires, banquets and parades gave The Eight a taste of vigorous life. This vigor showed in their color; it showed in their subject matter, barrooms, dead-end kids, New York's East Side; and, lastly, it came out in their preachings.

The Eight hit the sawdust trail of salvation in the alleyways of New York. Paint the life around you, they preached, and their prime sermonizer was Henri. Shooting epigram after epigram (they are collected by Margery Ryerson in *The Art Spirit*) at his students and followers, Henri put into words the hopes and determinations of this new order for America. That the artists were still largely European in style and technique; that they neither knew nor cared anything about the great hinterland behind and west of The Bronx that is the real America; that they still looked to Europe for the new in art— all these are beside the point. They were American in spirit. That is crystal clear in Luks' *The Spielers*, in Bellows' *Stag at Sharkey's*, in Sloan's *Wake of the Ferry No. 2*, even in the paintings of the impressionist members, Glackens and Lawson.

The Henri crowd had something else that was part of the American spirit. They were a "crowd"; they hung together; they were a school, if you please (as artists are in Paris when they hang together). But as men they were a confraternity, like a group of American newspapermen. And they were conscious, sometimes overly conscious as the years went by, of their clannishness.

This group, "the black revolutionary gang," set the stage for things that were to follow; they gave direction and leadership to American art, and offered a banner other than that of the National Academy for a new rally.

New York, by the end of the Twentieth Century's first decade, was a rapidly expanding organism. Physically it was growing, in population, buildings and maritime importance. Art in New York was also growing and nothing was better evidence of that fact than the artists' rising disdain for the Academy of Art. The National Academy had survived revolts. Disdain was new in its history.

The Chicago World's Fair of 1893 had spurred mural painting and Kenyon Cox and his fellow academicians were cashing in. The Academy did not see, and did not care, that the artist had an economic problem. Neither did it sense the increasing demand by the younger, coming artists for opportunity to exhibit. This was a demand that was to develop a whole industry of art dealers, who provided galleries and exhibition space. New York was becoming strongly art conscious. An exhibition by the Spaniard Sorolla in 1909 at the Hispanic Museum drew the largest audience (160,000) that has ever attended an art show by one man in the history of America. That was some indication of the temper of New York art circles. Sorolla's light went out as quickly as it came on, but at the time he drew a gate larger even than the surrealist Dali does today, with the best of press agents.

One other thing was in the New York air at this time: French modernism. Introductions to this new type of art could be obtained only at Alfred Steiglitz's Photo Secession Gallery. There the critics had their first glimpse of Matisse and Picasso. They also saw the work of a small band of Americans who were working in Paris in the French modernist style: Marin, Dasburg, Walkowitz, etc. But all this was to be seen at an address far off the beaten path, not even an art gallery but one that was dedicated to the radical theory that a photograph could be a work of art. Thus the stage was set: the comradeship of the Henri group and their liberating principles, a new disdain for the Academy, a general growing art interest in New York, and rumblings of a strange new modernism—an outlandish way of painting—over in France. Into that highly charged New York atmosphere a group of progressive American artists dropped a bombshell, then rather modestly catalogued as an "International Exhibition of Modern Art," but which lives today in art history as the famous Armory Show.

The Armory Show

The impact of modernism upon American art was like a high-powered explosion. It destroyed many of the old influences and fed into the stream of our art a vital current of simplicity and functionalism that is still evident, twenty-six years later, in the evolution of a native expression. The victory was not without its casualties. Many young Americans who mistook the surface perversions of modernism for its inner core have sacrificed their careers on the rocks of shallow thinking. The controversy between modernism and conservatism provided the art battle of the century, and, though the die-hards on both sides continue to die hard, victory has gone to neither. Compromise, as is so often the case, is now entrenched on the hard-fought field between the two camps. The Academy has accepted to a large extent the basic principles of modernism—simplification, honesty in the use of materials, elimination of extraneous detail and trite sentimentality. The vogue for ultramodern art has long since passed into the discard, with only the clever publicity machines of Paris standing between it and oblivion.

All this had its beginning in America with the Armory Show. For the American artist the Armory Show was the signing of a new declaration of independence from the tyranny of the Academy, the introduction of a new freedom that almost ruined him with its heady intoxication during the next few decades. For the general public the more evident effects of modernism may be seen in such adjuncts to living as streamlined automobiles and functional bathrooms. A bathtub is a receptacle in which to bathe. Why, asked the modern artist, shape it like a halved watermelon and mount it on claw-and-ball feet like grandma's dresser? An automobile is a mobile engine for rapid transit. Why stick to the design of grandpa's mauve-decade surrey? For these basic principles the public is in debt to the experimental achievements of the modern artists.

In architecture, industrial design, typography and poster art, modernism has marked a progressive milestone. In sculpture it produced, and is still producing, some of the century's greatest tactile masterpieces. In painting, however, it soared too high into the rarefied air of pure aesthetics, then degenerated into two-dimensional decorative art, or into "nonobjective" pictures better incorporated into textile designs than framed and hung on walls as examples of pictorial art. The years since the Armory Show have proved that American art could not assimilate the surface characteristics of such French modern painters as Picasso, Matisse, Dufy or Rouault—and remain American. On the other hand, those same years have seen American Scene painters absorb the fundamentals of modernism and produce a greater American art. Simplicity of form and functionalism of design are universal; the decorative and gay patterns of Matisse are personal to a Frenchman who, himself, got them second-hand from the Orient and imbued them with French taste and color.

There the line of demarcation must be drawn between the Frenchman and the American. Picasso during some of his multitudinous periods has gone back to Lekythos Greek vases and African gods; Rouault's paintings own up to their Coptic textile and medieval stained-glass inspiration; Modigliani shows a strange relationship between Sienese Madonnas and African sculptures; Paul Klee rummaged through antiquity to find kinship with Cro-Magnon cave scratchings; Dali has sophisticated the bizarre nightmares of the Dutchman Bosch. Beyond its basic principles there is little new in modernism. Should the American go to the same ancient sources, he would probably remain an American. When he imitates the imitations of the French moderns, he becomes a French modern, twice removed. Such have been the lessons of modernism which the Armory Show introduced to America the year before the Serb, Gavrilo Prinzip, killed an Austrian Archduke at Sarajevo.

The Armory Show was not planned as a bombshell. The idea originated with four young artists who had paintings but no public. They decided to rally together other artists in the same situation and to hold an exhibition of American art and, to add flavor and public appeal, they thought it would be smart to include some of the "new" art from abroad. As it eventually turned out, the side show—the French modernism from abroad—stole the show, but in stealing it the committee's original hope was realized. America was given a jolt.

An account of the Armory Show has, fortunately, been written within the past few years by Walt Kuhn, the man most closely connected with it from start to finish. In his small pamphlet, *The Story of the Armory Show*, Kuhn has re-created some of the excitement and enthusiasm of that event a quarter-century ago and has set aright the record for all time. He writes:

"Two things produced the Armory Show: a burning desire by everyone to be informed of the slightly known activities abroad and the need for breaking down the stifling and smug condition of local art affairs as applied to the ambitions of American painters and sculptors. This was the one point. The other was the lucky discovery of a leader well equipped with the necessary knowledge of art and a self-sacrificing and almost unbelievable sporting attitude. This was the American painter Arthur B. Davies. As put forth in his manifesto in the catalogue, our purpose was solely to show the American people what was going on abroad, but this was only a half-truth. The real truth was that the Armory Show developed into a genuine, powerful and, judging from results, most effective revolt, perhaps even more effective than the incident of the Salon des Refuses of Paris in 1864. The group of four men who set the wheels in motion had no idea of the magnitude to which their early longings would lead. Perhaps they felt just one thing—that something had to be done to insure them a chance to breathe."

The four men were Kuhn, Elmer McRae, Jerome Myers, all artists, and Henry Fitch Taylor, director of a small gallery conducted by Mrs. Clara Potter Davidge which gave free exhibitions to young artists.

It was in December, 1911, that the group, sitting ruefully about in the empty gallery where their pictures hung, hit upon the Armory Show idea. They called in more similarly situated artists, several of them conservatives, and formed the Association of American Painters and Sculptors, with Davies at the head, J. Mowbray Clarke as vice-president, Walt Kuhn as secretary and Elmer McRae as treasurer. Other members were Karl Anderson, George Bellows, D. Putnam Brinley, Leon Dabo, Jo Davidson, Guy Pène du Bois, Sherry E. Fry, William J. Glackens, Robert Henri, E. A. Kramer, Ernest Lawson, Jonas Lie (the first of Lie's three revolts against the Academy he now heads), George Luks, Jerome Myers, Frank A. Nankivell, Bruce Potter, Maurice Prendergast, John Sloan, Henry Fitch Taylor, Allen Tucker and Mahonri Young. It will be noticed that seven of The Eight—Davies, Glackens, Henri, Lawson, Luks, Prendergast and Sloan—were among these "rebels" who were to halt the growth of the Henri group which had already begun to develop an American Scene art.

The show opened at the 69th Regiment Armory in New York on February 15, 1913, with adequate, but uninteresting notices from the critics. The exhibition languished for a week. Then something happened—the city editors, hearing of a "freak" show, had sent their news reporters not their critics to cover it. The public stormed the Armory Show. Thousands of persons suddenly made it their duty to see these "crazy" works of art by Europeans. "Cubism" became a journalistic word. Reporters came in every day for a new angle of humor. Former President Roosevelt attended and condemned the entire proceedings to the lunatic fringe. For one month the Armory Show was the main topic of conversation in New York art circles. The public misunderstood and hated modernism. Others, those who had been working in Paris with the moderns, tried to explain the movement to the public. Walter Pach lectured; James Gregg wrote; the artists talked. Matisse, Cézanne, Lehmbruck, Duchamp, Picasso and others were reviled, scourged by the public and the academic artists. The Frenchman Picabia (he was more in the news than Picasso) came rushing to America to cash in on the publicity. Marcel Duchamp's *Nude Descending the Stairs*, renamed *Cyclone in a Shingle Factory*, became the popular symbol of this crazy new art. The show moved on to Chicago and Boston, where more curses were heaped on it and where more yards of newsprint were devoted to art. Matisse and Brancusi were ridiculed in effigy by the students of the Art Institute of Chicago. (Students of this same institution have just now rendered a similar honor to the conservative critic of the Chicago *Tribune*, Eleanor Jewett, who dared to criticize their lack of academic craftsmanship.)

Nothing more wholesome could have happened to American art. The Armory Show became a public, national event. No other art exhibition in America before or since has achieved that distinction and, though French modernism ran away with the publicity honors, all of art gained. Art became something for the public to reckon with, something to argue about. It became front-page news.

In perspective the effects of the Armory Show have been both beneficial and detrimental. This attempt of a few American artists to find a public outlet introduced modern French art to their home audience, encouraged such pioneer collectors of modern art as John Quinn and Lillie Bliss and, eventually, resulted in providing France with its richest art market. In the wake of this encouragement have come the high-geared publicity machinery of foreign-art merchandising and the fascinating game of international art politics. There has come also the destruction of the average American's confidence in his own judgment. On the other hand, American museums have been enriched by the best of French art, and from the adventure American artists have obtained a new freedom in technique.

Lately the French modern school has slipped into an applied art with close affiliations to industry. And it is this angle that the Museum of Modern Art is now pushing as it pins the badge of fine art upon motion pictures, Walt Disney's animated cartoons, tubular furniture and travel posters. Yet, in spite of the current vogue for applied art, easel painting can still carry a great message. An empty canvas still remains a challenge to equal the great Rembrandt; it remains the most personal, most individual vehicle by which man can express the deepest, finest feelings of his inner being.

Since much of modern art was unexplainable even by the artists without the assistance of trained translators, the Armory Show started a group of esoteric art critics, spurred by Clive Bell and Roger Fry, to writing about art in a language that was beyond the understanding of the average intelligent person. Dr. Albert C. Barnes, master of the finest collection of modern French art in America, is the greatest present-day exponent of this intricate business of bewildering the layman. The "Analyses" appended to his volume on *The Art of Henri Matisse* stands as a monument to the difficult task of reading meaning into a picture where the artist meant none to exist.

Matisse painted a minor canvas back in 1917 of a distorted blue villa set amid a sketchy landscape, but to Dr. Barnes "the movement and pattern of curvilinear units which prevail in all four sections bind together the contrasting aspects in an uninterrupted flow of color-rhythms which encompass the central building. At each corner of this undulatory frame, the contrasts are greatly reduced by the intermediary transitional relationships."

No wonder a word-weary art public, resentful at being treated as yokels, welcomed with open arms the readable and intelligent columns of our contemporary art critics, who week after week labor to gain for art a wider circle of appreciators. In the field of art criticism the subsequent effect of the Armory Show has been decidedly beneficial.

Another effect of the Armory Show was to present every American artist with the problem of a crossroad: should he ignore French modernism, copy it, assimilate it? Ernest Lawson, Harry Watrous, Charles Hopkinson, Childe Hassam, Frank Nankivell, among others, ignored it. Arthur B. Davies, John Sloan and Alfred Maurer were among those checked by it. Leon Kroll, Eugene Speicher, George Biddle, Kenneth Hayes Miller and William Zorach are a few who compromised with it. Edward Hopper, Walt Kuhn, Charles Burchfield, Yasuo Kuniyoshi and Charles Sheeler are among those who assimilated it.

After the Armory Show came the World War, and its effect on American art, as on so many other phases of American life, was disastrous. The War upset the economic structure of the nation, checked all cultural development in the mad nightmare of destruction and, on the reaction of jazz emotionalism, gave strength to the growth of American left-wing art. It was the heyday of internationalism. Our bankers were syphoning off the billions to Europe. Our artists were sopping up cubism, futurism, dadaism or any other stylish ism they could find except Americanism. Cézanne, Picasso, Matisse, Gauguin, Modigliani were hailed as the giants of all time. Riding the crest of the wave among New York intellectuals were John Marin, Arthur Dove, Charles Demuth, Maurice Sterne, Preston Dickinson, Stuart Davis, Joseph Stella, Abraham Walkowitz, Max Weber and Man Ray.

With the aftermath of the World War came nationalism in American art—the return from Bohemia of Thomas Benton, John Steuart Curry and Grant Wood. This was the rise of the American Scene, a logical step after the disillusionment of the War, the shattering of Wilsonian ideals, the matter of war debts and the growing distrust of Machiavellian diplomacy. The wave of French modernism had spent its force by late 1929; its leaders were already turning from abstract experiments to more conservative representation; and America, for once in step with the times, saw the handwriting on the wall.

The Rise of Nationalism

The nationalization of American art is by far the most significant art movement of the present decade. It has been a natural evolution of a great people. The Dutch influence of Colonial days, the English tradition of Copley and West, the French romanticism of Vanderlyn, the Turner, Constable and Barbizon influences on our landscape school, the Munich darkness of Duveneck, the Yankee objectivism of Homer, the poetic imagination of Ryder, the broken color of the impressionists, the "ashcan" viewpoint of The Eight, and the modernism of the Armory Show—all these bewildering currents and crosscurrents were obligatory before America could learn to walk alone. These were all part of our internship. Today, as Europe stands in danger of seeing her art become anemic, through internal dissension and rumors of war, America confidently accepts the challenge of the future.

The immediate causes at the base of America's emergence as a world power in art are: first, the American Scene school of painting, bred of politico-economic nationalism and the concurrent resentment against the high-pressure dumping of inferior foreign art on the home market; second, the progressive amalgamation of modernism and conservatism, together with the more recent wedding of American Scene painting and "Pure Art"; and, third, the entry of the Federal government into art at a time when the depression had dried up the old wells of patronage by the wealthy, leisure class. Each of these phases will be treated at greater length in the pages to follow.

The intense nationalism that now guides American art owes its beginnings in part to economic and political conditions, in part to the traditional European misconception of American thought and character. At its core, of course, lies Europe's contention that Americans are incapable of producing an art of their own and must, consequently, remain a consumer market for the more artistic citizens of the Old World. To be born in America, they reason, must automatically remove from the unfortunate babe those qualities of sensitivity and fineness of fiber that make an artist. America, they argue, is rough, vulgar, still molested by Indians who shoot flint-tipped arrows from the ramparts of the Palisades. What if America was first colonized when Rembrandt was a boy? America, at all costs, must continue as Dodsworth's wife to art-producing nations.

Acceleration to the patriotic "Paint American" and "Buy American" movement came after the War. As the grip of adversity tightened about the nation, Americans suddenly came back to reality, came once again to rely upon their own resources. Self-sufficiency was the order of the day, and this contributed largely to the founding of the new school of art, the American School, which becomes stronger the farther away it can get from contemporary European influences. Thus American art as it exists today came from and of the people—and art once again lived up to its historic role in expressing the feelings and thoughts of a people. Our youngsters have deserted the ateliers of Paris to seek at home their art training; our art lovers, no longer proud of their imported taste, have discovered that America may possess artists as great as any age or race has produced. We have found our Old Masters in Homer, Ryder and Eakins, and look to our contemporaries for the Old Masters of the future.

Nationalism has supplied the one missing design from the pattern of our artistic life. Despite the warnings of internationalists against flag waving and their arguments that great art is universal, not nationalistic, the age-old natural law that art must first be national before it can be universal has once again been proved.

The nationalist Rembrandt never visited Italy, exclaiming as he painted his universal paintings of Seventeenth-Century Holland, "You can learn to paint at home." All art history demonstrates that great art has been a perfect expression of the nationalism, or national unity, of the people that produced it. We can point to Egyptian, Hindu, Assyrian, Greek, Gothic and Renaissance art as inevitable and fit products of the political, economic, intellectual and spiritual life of their creators. Though certain identical aesthetic elements, certain immortal qualities are akin and therefore universal, nationalism has always first given them voice and must always remain the first aspect of all lasting art. To be a great artist one must be able to feel; to feel one must be able to touch.

Another irritant contributing to the drift of the American artist into his present state of forthright nationalism was his old grievance against the European portraitist, usually a third-rate member of the pretty-pretty school of eyelash affixers, who crosses the Atlantic to batten on portrait commissions from the culturally illiterate. These "artists" are merely commercial limners, skillful in surface flashiness and clever masters of the technique of publicity and social flattery. Americans who try to click heels with them usually end up on an elbow. The news and society reporters (not the art critics) give them yards of publicity with photographs dramatizing their records among European royalty. A visit to Washington would produce sittings from Congressmen, a member of the Cabinet or even the President —every American ruler since 1912, except F.D.R., patiently sat to some foreign painter, for "reasons of state." After a year among our dollar aristocrats, the "artist" would carry back across the Atlantic with him as much as $50,000—his departure attended by the futile curses of better but less suave American portraitists. It is a condition that obtains even today. American taste in the upper brackets being what it is, our lords and ladies of breeding and position like to feel that the same brush that painted Duchess Thisque or Countess Thatque can be hired by Mrs. Smith to outshine Mrs. Jones.

Still another thing that irritated the American art world and spurred nationalism was the subtle propaganda and supersalesmanship of the Paris art merchants, who thus built up a collectors' cult. This cult, artificially nourished through esoteric art writings and not a few rigged auctions, would not even consider the native product, but would gulp down with evident relish the studio sweepings of any well-publicized French modern. Most American artists knew even then that the bulk of this hasty hack painting, imported with impressive fanfare, would twenty years later not be worth the cost of the frames. But their voices went unheeded. It angered the native artist and his patron, drew them closer together in the nationalism that was finding expression in the American Scene movement.

The temper of the times was well illustrated by the reception accorded Gertrude Stein's so-called opera, a work in paranoiac participles that was proposed to be brilliant because it was beyond the ken of man or god. Miss Stein, reputed to be the modern genius of letters by her fellow expatriates in Paris, called her opus *Three Saints in Four Acts*, or was it *Four Saints in Three Acts?* It does not much matter. The well-oiled machinery of international publicity was thrown into high gear. The New York intellectuals and the Hartford Group of advanced thinkers trembled with excitement. The reporters had their usual field day with the incomprehensible Stein verses. The art public—and here is where the previously effective machinery broke down—smiled with quiet amusement and argued about Tom Benton's murals. Back to Paris went the Three (or Four) Saints together with Miss Stein, who, for all America knows, still sits with the pigeons on the grass alas the pigeons on the grass alas.

Thus the reaction caused by the incessant French propaganda, by the very law of compensation, helped in the development of an American School, gave impetus to the American Scene type of painting.

The American Scene

It was less than ten years ago that this tidal wave of nationalistic feeling surged over the civilized world to send peoples and nations scurrying back to their origins and their native traditions. In politics it was as deadly as the plague; in art it produced, on the whole, a healthy condition. For example, as this return to the indigenous took on different complexions in different countries, it ranged from the violent tragico-ludicrous saber rattling of Europe's three dictators to the rise of a fruitful school of painting in the United States. Out of it came, in American art, the American Scene group, based solidly on nationalism and its subdivision, regionalism.

This was the most healthy development in the entire three hundred years of American art history. The artist literally returned to the soil for his subject material and traveled as far away as possible from foreign isms. He stepped down from his ivory tower and out into the fields, the streets and the factories. Though his brush too frequently served only the ugliness of American life, the native painter had succeeded in dropping his last chains of French serfdom. The decks were swept clear, as the American discovered in some Midwestern tank town or New England textile mill the same powerful urge to create that Gauguin sought in exotic Tahiti and poor, mad Van Gogh found in windswept Arles. The American artist had come home.

As the movement gained momentum more and more of America's artists discovered paintable America through realistic observation of the everyday life about them. Long-forgotten American artists were resurrected, and it became evident that American Scene painting has had a continual, slowly evolving tradition in the United States since the days of Homer and Bingham, of Bellows and Sloan. And the public was appreciative. Not just a small group of initiated aesthetes, but an ever-widening circle of "common people" saw in the familiar subjects and homespun sentiments something they knew and loved. The internationalists howled, contemptuously dubbed the American Sceners "graphic artists," and thoroughly misunderstood the signs of the times. Nationwide publicity helped bring American Scene painting an extraordinary popularity. And as the general public lost its suspicions of "crazy modernism" and "long-haired bohemians," it dropped its indifference and began to take a real interest in native art.

Pioneers in the American Scene movement, even before it claimed its popular title, were Charles Burchfield and Edward Hopper. Burchfield, who is to art what Sinclair Lewis is to American letters, paints Main Street with gentle satire. Memory, in our maturity, has the power to halo with beauty the most ugly objects of our boyhood. This is the secret behind the nostalgic appeal of the Syracuse Museum's Burchfield, *Six o'Clock* (Page 47), and the Metropolitan Museum's *November*. Hopper, more austere and less personal than Burchfield, is also a sympathetic recorder of melancholy architecture (see *House by the Railroad*, Page 123), but his favorite subjects are deserted city streets and unpeopled restaurants and movie theatres. Another pioneer is James Chapin, who for several years, on a farm near Flemington, N. J., found ideal material for his powerful series of rural subjects and immortalized the Marvin family as they sat humbly about their kitchen range. Painter of the American Babbitt and the sophisticated debutante to perfection is Guy Pène du Bois, man of many talents who belongs to the movement only through his indigenous point of view.

Then like a clap of thunder came the now famous Midwest Trinity of American Scene painters— John Steuart Curry of Kansas, Thomas Hart Benton of Missouri and Grant Wood of Iowa. Their renown, sweeping the country almost overnight, marked the true beginning of a revolt, the final effects of which have not yet been realized. Indeed this movement is now becoming international. Homer Saint-Gaudens, director of fine arts at Pittsburgh's Carnegie Institute, recently returned from a tour of Europe's art centers and said: "I find that subject is again returning in painting to support quality or harmony. This is a healthful sign, as the quality of painting is made interesting by the variety of expressions, in other words, subjects."

Curry, with a vigorous, dynamic brush, caught the spirit of his environment in *Baptism in Kansas* (Page 73), and in *Tornado over Kansas* (Page 71) gave vivid conception to the common fear of man and beast in the face of nature's destructive forces. Benton, seeking to know America at first hand, traversed the South and the West, studying life in the Bible Belt, along the unconquered Mississippi and in the farm lands of Missouri. He painted such folk subjects as *The Jealous Lover of Lone Green Valley* (Page 68). Wood's *American Gothic*, sympathetically satirizing the Iowa farmer (Page 65), set the pace for the American Scene when it won an important prize at the Chicago Art Institute. Later his *Daughters of Revolution* (Page 66), holding up to ridicule the snobbery of the old historic aristocracy, became an American classic and the stampede back to the soil was on.

The one dominating trend of the present decade of American art—the 1930s—has been this return to the soil, the painting of the American Scene in all its fascinating facets. The movement, pioneered by Curry, Benton and Wood, caught the imagination of artists, young and veteran alike, and by the closing years of the '30s had assumed the proportions of an irresistible force—with no immovable object in sight.

Painter after painter discarded his trite concern with studio nudes, with a vase of flowers, or a still life with mandolin. He fared forth on the highways and byways of America or he returned to his boyhood habitat and painted the subjects that had subconsciously thrilled his heart. A fascinating panorama unfolded. America is a vast physical area with not one but a thousand aspects. It is a variegated, mosaiclike picture in which the parts add up to the sum of the whole. Benton demonstrated this in his Whitney Museum mural when, cinema-like, he threw upon the walls of that great museum, dedicated through the generosity of Gertrude Vanderbilt Whitney and the wisdom of Juliana Force to the greater glory of American art, a flickering cross section of America. There are gangsters, bankers, cowboys and torch singers—all in one picture.

But the individual pieces of America's great mosaic have been the artists' greatest concern. Each has staked out his claim, and has his own preserve of subject matter.

In New York City Reginald Marsh paints the crowds of Coney Island and the inhibited audiences of burlesque shows with, as in *High Yaller* (Page 81), an occasional glance at picturesque characters outlined against the once-impressive brown-stone fronts. The younger Paul Cadmus, when he is not twitting the admirals, paints vulgar aspects of metropolitan play, as in *Coney Island* (Page 100). Louis Guglielmi paints with understanding the hordes of New York's East Side. When they go shopping along Fourteenth Street, Kenneth Hayes Miller, who will probably go down in history as a great teacher, lies in wait to paint them. Near by, at the close of day as high-school girls of the city linger to tell each other secrets, Isabel Bishop sketches.

Out in the Midwest, in addition to the three pioneers of Kansas, Missouri and Iowa, the nation's grain farmers are watched by Ogden Pleissner, John De Martelly and Joe Jones. The silos of Ohio are recorded with imaginative vigor by Clarence Carter. In Texas the tragedy of soil erosion is Alexandre Hogue's message in such canvases as *Drouth-Stricken Area* (Page 75), while life in the Ozarks is the special domain of Everett Spruce. Depicting the Southwest generally are Jerry Bywaters and William Lester. Along the California Sierras and on the ranches roams Millard Sheets; down along the San Francisco docks may be found Maynard Dixon. Among the New Mexico pueblos Ernest Blumenschein, Kenneth Adams, Theodore Van Soelen, Victor Higgins and Emil Bisttram paint and live. Out in the cattle country Peter Hurd paints the pinon-studded hillsides as in *The Dry River* (Page 77). The landscapes of Colorado hold John E. Thompson, sensitive advocate of regionalism. Frank Mechau makes rhythmic designs of the few remaining wild horses of the West. The atmosphere of California is caught in the water colors of Tom Craig, Phil Paradise, Phil Dike and S. MacDonald Wright.

The rooftops of Philadelphia furnish patterns for Antonio Martino. Francis Speight paints the rural Pennsylvania, Daniel Garber its trees, and John Folinsbee finds beauty along the canal at New Hope. Paul Sample gives a genre view of a *Janitor's Holiday* (Page 75), and Barse Miller takes life as he finds it, at a beach party or in a Model T Ford. Investigating the nation's industrial centers are Charles Sheeler (see *City Interior*, Page 126), Paul Meltsner and many others. At a ball game you may see Paul Clemens, at the race track Lee Townsend, at the Yale Bowl, Benton Spruance. Behind the sagebrush of the desert lurks Otis Dozier; in Vermont's Green Mountains, Edward Bruce or Luigi Lucioni (see his *Vermont Classic*, Page 101). Down in Alabama, where steel mills have piled mountains of waste upon the landscape, is Lamar Dodd; up in Rockport the romantic Jon Corbino is at the height of his power in such pictures as *Flood Refugees* (Page 45).

Wherever there is American life there is an artist. Before city planning cleans up Chicago, its pungently ugly side streets and outlying districts are haunted by Aaron Bohrod (Page 104). In New Orleans John McCrady puts on canvas his conception of the Negro spiritual, *Swing low, Sweet Chariot* (Page 99). On a Provincetown wharf is Ross Moffett; in the valley near Woodstock, Ernest Fiene, Emil Ganso (Page 128), Judson Smith, or Georgina Klitgaard (Page 128). Henry Mattson paints the symbol of the sea's power, while Frederick Waugh, most popular of marine painters, gives it realistic meaning. (Contrast *Night and the Sea* on Page 127 with *The Big Water* on Page 125). Rural courtship intrigues Doris Lee in *Noon* (Page 48).

This list of subjects, the small pieces of mosaic, seems endless. From the admittedly incomplete enumeration already given it becomes obvious that the American Scene is an ever-changing total of infinite local scenes. It becomes obvious that American Scene painting is in reality regionalism in art, fragments of the American panorama best known to the individual native artists.

The American Scene has been a remarkable development in the story of American art; one with a profound influence upon artist and public alike. A new, tingling sense of participation has come to the public—to the workers in the factories, to the cowhands in the West, to those who love the land on which they live and the people with whom they mingle. This mutual affection for America and things American has brought a greater communion between artist and public.

Twenty years ago the average American considered it the mission of art to depict only what is beautiful on the surface. Fostered by the Academy and the pseudoclassic painters of Europe, the public came to the attitude that art must deal solely with the pretty—with sunsets, Bouguereau nudes, impressionistic vistas, or with the allegorical handling of an outworn Greek myth. Educated to this preference, the public could easily understand the classification of Henri's group as the "Ashcan School."

But when Curry and Benton and Wood took the bit in their teeth, foreswore the studio flower arrangements and the posed studio still lifes, the public received its greatest lesson in American history. It was taught, and with a jolt, that art arises wherever there are artists. Art is wedded to no tight little set of subjects painted over and over in Paris. It learned that Paris was unimportant.

Like all great revolts in art, the American Scene had its drawbacks as well as its advantages. At first something of a "cult of ugliness" was built up, as too many artists, painting at the top of their voices, argued that "ugliness is strength, beauty is weakness." They forgot, as one painter phrased it, that "the 'pansy' and the 'gorilla' are both necessary in any work of art, the one to lend taste, the other to supply force." The American Scene fostered among certain artists a ridiculous non sequitur: the theory that a painting of an American subject automatically assures an American painting to be the result. It fostered, also, a certain attitude of jingoism, a Yankee Doodle bravado among other artists who, hating Europe and its modern art, were only too glad of the opportunity to junk all of Europe's advances in aesthetics.

But those bad effects of the American Scene movement were far outweighed by one great influence for the good—it released the artists' spirits, broadened their horizons, and unrolled a vast new field for their expression. In a word, it let down the stifling barriers that the Academy, the Salon and the School of Paris had put around art.

Nothing in the world is a more sensitive record of human emotions and convictions than a painting. If an artist likes celery he may put it in his painting, endowing it with those qualities he likes about it, its crunchy freshness and crispness or its rather gay form. But under the regime of the School of Paris and the Academy alike, American artists were restricted in their freedom to record their deepest emotions. The Academy would deny the artist the freedom to paint his celery. Instead, it dictated a picturesque scene or a pseudoclassic figure composition. The School of Picasso, Matisse and the other French moderns dictated the Pure Art forms of subjects that appeal to Frenchmen—the accouterments of bohemian life on the Left Bank. Under the sway of the Parisian moderns, it may be argued, any painter was free to depict, if he wanted, the folks back home in Kansas or a scene in Klein's Department Store on Fourteenth Street. Theoretically he was free to do so, practically he was not.

Contrast the narrow gamut of subject matter that was painted by the Paris moderns with the subjects briefly enumerated in the list of American Scene painters previously mentioned. Consider the importance of such a widening of the American artists' horizon—the opening of a whole new continent of the spirit. In the light of this effect the few bad results of the American Scene movement pale into insignificance. The band of Curry, Benton and Wood was like a Lewis and Clark expedition into the realm of the emotions.

Social Protest

The rise of the social segment of the American Scene was a product of the depression decade, as the artist, striking back blindly at life, embraced left-wing philosophy as the road to economic security. One can starve more gracefully if the mind is fed with dreams of a coming Utopia. Paint was their weapon, and they viciously fought the system they hated by caricaturing the bleaker aspects of contemporary society.

For all its amateur fellow travelers, it cannot be denied that this division of American Scene painting produced some canvases of lasting merit. These are by professional artists who commented upon the obvious defects of modern industrial society with considerable beauty and with singular clarity of thought. Their eager participation in the social problems of their times lent them added power. Artists are predominantly liberal in their views, quick to react to the suffering of their fellows. The depression dramatized misery for them and they were eager to crusade against want in the midst of plenty. Propaganda, in the broad sense of the term, is as old as art itself. The early Italians painted religious propaganda and were paid for it; Rembrandt with every subtle brush stroke preached tolerance; Goya, without employing any screaming banners, lampooned the degenerate ruling class of Spain.

In this volume may be seen four paintings of social significance by sensitive, fine artists who used their talent to give permanent value to their propagandic messages. They are *Arrest No. 2* by Henry Billings (Page 103); *Doctor's Office* by Raphael Soyer (Page 105); *The Senate* by William Gropper (Page 104); and the government mural *Tenement* by George Biddle (Page 102). Their messages ring clear, and they demonstrate what the true artist can do with propaganda when he does not forget art. Other contemporary artists who have painted powerful social documents include Aaron Bohrod, Arnold Blanch, George Picken, Maynard Dixon, Mervin Jules, Manuel Tolegian, Edward Millman, Fletcher Martin, Francis Criss, Frank Kirk, Julian Levi, Jack Markow, Jack Levine and Louis Guglielmi. Dixon's *Destination Unknown*, graphic in conception, is a great social document of the past decade, great because it is a simple, sincere statement—a lone figure of a beaten, but undefeated man trudging the ties of a railroad that extends out into the vast unknown future.

Social Protest painting as we know it today appears to have been an outgrowth peculiar to the current depression and an indication that the artists are more aware of their times. Our earlier artists painted no records of the depressions of 1873 and 1893, made no comments on the great Pullman strike or the tragic struggle of the steel workers at Homestead. Neither did they pay any attention to the Populist, Free Silver or any of the other lunatic movements before California cried for "ham and eggs" and Dr. Townsend appealed to America's elderly multitude. The nearest relative of Social Protest is the old *Masses*, the magazine which provided an outlet for the "socialistic" cartoons of Boardman Robinson, Bellows, Henri and Sloan.

The main weakness of the Social Protest group lies in its host of parlor-pink camp followers, painters who cannot paint but who see in the class struggle a Cause—something firm on which to anchor for a fleeting moment their dangling thoughts. With the average laborer their feeble attempts to imitate French modernism or German expressionism may raise a smile but never a revolution. These failures, on whom must rest the decline of the group, are probably sincere in their own lights, but sincerity was never an adequate excuse for bad painting.

A New Trend—Pure Art

The first flush of the American Scene has passed. Today, among America's best artists, the matter of painting a subject local to the artist has become an accepted freedom and they are going into the newest development of contemporary American painting, a concern for what we shall call Pure Art. This is perhaps the culmination of our native school, the climax of a slow evolution that began back in the late 1600s with the arrival from London of John Smibert, Hogarth's fellow student, and continued through the many influences outlined earlier in this book.

The exciting new phase retains the freedom and nationalistic strength of the American Scene, but places greater emphasis on the aesthetics of painting. It is, in a sense, a counter revolt from the local color and too obvious dependence upon subject of the average American Scener. Texture, design, color organization, form, paint quality and a deeper feeling for media are claiming more attention as the native artist becomes more accustomed to his newly won freedom.

Signs of this greater concentration upon aesthetic problems have been in the air for a longer time than most of us realize. Each summer the Toledo Museum holds an important exhibition of contemporary American paintings, carefully selected to illustrate the latest developments. This small but select exhibition is always thoroughly in tune with the times. This year cognizance of the trend toward Pure Art was given by the director when he said in the catalogue foreword:

"The development in technique of many of the known men will be noted as well as the effort of some of the later artists to develop new mediums of representation. Our own feeling is that the best Americans have passed the stage of experimentation and are now stressing pure painting. After all, this is the rock on which America must eventually rest if she is to give any real contribution to art history, and not on propaganda or the various isms with which Europe has been belabored."

The swing to Pure Art is well defined by the five reproductions on pages 68, 69, and 70 of early and late paintings by Thomas Benton, famous American Scene pioneer. First of these paintings is *The Jealous Lover of Lone Green Valley*, painted in 1930 in the heyday of American Scenism. *Huck Finn and Nigger Jim*, part of the Missouri State House mural, and *T. P. and Jake*, dated 1936 and 1937, come next, while the latest period in Benton's art is represented by *Pussy Cat and Roses* and the nude *Persephone*. Even a casual study of these five pictures will show that Benton, working and thinking out in Missouri, has changed his style, matured his technique and enriched his color.

Benton, archapostle of the American factual scene, is now painting lush still lifes, simple landscapes and symbolic nudes that, with more subtle diction, still illustrate the pageant of America. Benton, archexponent of hard, Grecoesque forms and broad areas of design, is now engrossed in the painting of minute details. Finally and most significant, Benton, who cared nothing for texture, is painting the luxuriant surfaces of leaves, trees, flesh and fabrics—and he is painting them only for their *feel*.

The change is best seen in *Persephone* (Page 69), a figure of a nude reclining in a secluded rural Missouri spot amid rich vegetation. Her privacy is about to be violated by a horny-handed old farmer, custodian of the distant plentiful fields. The implication is despoliation of the land by the American farmer. In classic literature Persephone was the goddess of nature and of abundance. In this modern version of the Rape of Persephone, Benton is scoring the greed of those who cultivate the land to exhaustion, to the point of drouths, erosion and dust storms. It is still "American Scene."

Subtlety is the keynote to Benton's new manner. His color, creating an actual light through the entire area of his canvases, is used to give a complete sculptural life to each of the many forms, to play over the new-found textures. The old linear hardness of the figures has been softened; the surface is distinguished for its finished appearance. In his new certainty and delight with painting, Benton reflects self-assurance and retains his wholesome American flavor.

What Benton has done scores of other American Scene painters have done or are doing in America today. It is the most thrilling promise that the future holds.

The Government Enters Art

"It must be admitted that for the overwhelming majority of the American people the fine arts of painting and sculpture in their non-commercial, non-industrial forms, do not exist."

Such were the barren findings of two experts assigned by President Hoover in 1930 to study the arts in American life.

Now move up the years—to June 1939:

"Despite the uncertainty, the unsettled conditions, the state of affairs all about us, here in America opportunities such as never before could be found welcome the artist on every hand. The artist is being lifted out of the relatively small luxury class. He is being assigned, if I may put it so, to the people."

These words, spoken to the graduating class of the Yale Art School by Edward Alden Jewell, express succinctly the main trend of the art world today. In the seven years between 1932 and 1939 American art underwent the greatest transformation in its history.

One reason is that the United States government, for the first time in its history, stepped into the arena of art patronage and joined the old line capitalists there. The idea of art and literature and music is deeply ingrained in the American mind. Modern English literature never produced a best seller like *Main Street* or *Babbitt*. These books were great and popular protests against America's dullness about culture—and the fact that they swept the country, sold a half million each, shows that the negative of their charge met an equally positive force in the minds of the U.S.A. public.

The New Deal gave a spurt to art. But the art and will for liking art were there first. Old line

American Gothic—GRANT WOOD

Daughters of Revolution—Grant Wood

Woman with Plants—GRANT WOOD

The Jealous Lover of Lone Green Valley—THOMAS HART BENTON

Persephone—THOMAS HART BENTON

Huck Finn and Nigger Jim—Thomas Hart Benton

T. P. and Jake—Thomas Hart Benton

Pussy Cat and Roses—Thomas Hart Benton

Tornado over Kansas—John Steuart Curry

Line Storm—John Steuart Curry

Circus Elephants—John Steuart Curry

Baptism in Kansas—JOHN STEUART CURRY

The Corn Dance—Edward Laning

Janitor's Holiday—PAUL SAMPLE

Drouth-Stricken Area—ALEXANDRE HOGUE

Corner Grocery, Taos—WARD LOCKWOOD

Dead Head—EDWIN L. FULWIDER

Boy from the Plains—PETER HURD

The Dry River—PETER HURD

The Country Doctor—Lauren Ford

Maine Trotting Race—Waldo Peirce

New England Harbor—EDNA REINDEL

Transfer of Mail from Liner to Tugboat—Reginald Marsh

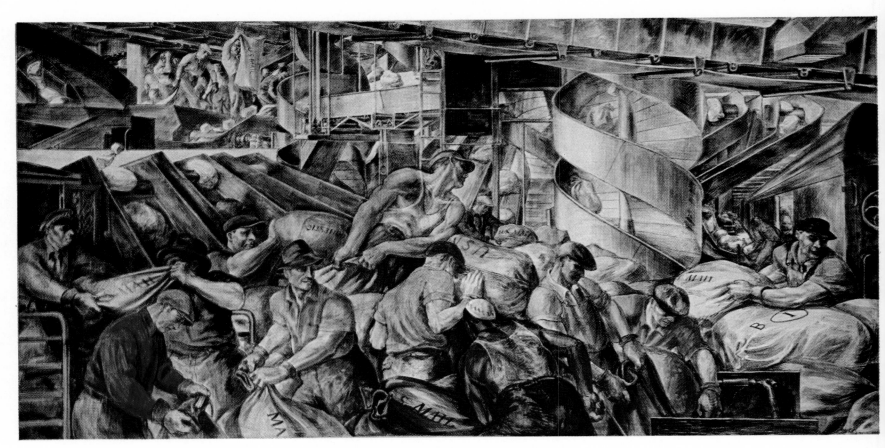

Sorting Mail—Reginald Marsh

High Yaller—REGINALD MARSH

TVA Worker and Family   *Pleading the Gold Case*   *Custom House Workers*   *Surveying New Lands*

HENRY VARNUM POOR

capitalists and the New Deal have always been on the side of art. But art is greater than government or individual patronage. The government has made as many mistakes in taste as the Republican capitalists, but the government's sense of direction in public liking was better. The best thing the government did was to inspire local state and community feeling. Private fortunes have helped there too: with the result a boom in art feeding a natural hunger of a nation. No one agency alone did it: the government and the Old Guard both played into the people's yearnings.

But the government went back to the Renaissance for a model in its patronage. At the lowest point of the nation's worst economic plight Uncle Sam, once thoroughly and completely disinterested in art, extended two enfolding arms to the artists of America. One was the Treasury Department's Section of Fine Art. The other, the Federal Art Project. It did not put the artists on a dole. It paid them for creating art for the state.

The cry of Renaissance raised, then questioned, in the first chapter of this book, is a cry that rises spontaneously when America is seated with the company of the Medici, the Pharaohs and the Greeks. But sober restraint demands a quick distinction. Uncle Sam ranks with the illustrious group quantitatively. No one dares yet say *qualitatively*.

America went into art patronage haltingly, experimentally, and in the beginning not for the reason of art but for relief. The major problem facing President Roosevelt when he took office in 1933 was alleviation of unemployment. When this problem was most acute, two ex-classmates from Harvard—Edward Bruce and George Biddle—approached the President with a plan for the relief of artists. Artists had been virtually unemployed for several years previous to the national emergency. Art was a luxury; the luxuries were the first to suffer. John Sloan once dramatized their plight in a cartoon which showed a banker scrambling into a shell hole labeled "The Depression." Turning around, the banker noticed an artist and exclaimed, "What! You here too?"

"This is my home," replied the artist.

It was to get the artist out of his shell hole and at the same time enrich the nation culturally that the government first entered art. Within the structure of the CWA, the first great work relief project, a division called PWAP (Public Works of Art Project) was established. In one year it hired 3,000 needy artists to make government murals and other decorations. The division was headed by Edward Bruce, a lawyer turned artist, a man trained to act swiftly in an emergency. At the same time, Bruce is an idealist who knows the spiritual values. It can be well said that without Bruce and his peculiar combination of talents no lasting Federal program in art would have been launched. Forbes Watson, adviser to the government's Section of Fine Arts, credits him with placing the United States "in the lead as a country more intent upon the welfare of its artists than any other country," and calls him "the fountainhead of all that the United States has done for art in the past five years."

Bruce's PWAP adventure was short-lived. It was soon realized that the nation faced not only a relief problem but also a cultural one. Relief for artists was then transformed into the Federal Art Project of the WPA, with Holger Cahill as its national head. Bruce was authorized to set up within the Treasury Department a Section of Fine Arts, whose function would have nothing to do with relief. It was charged with the responsibility of procuring for Federal buildings the best possible art by the nation's best artists, known and unknown. To execute this duty efficiently and with no favoritism, a system of regional competitions was evolved. When inventory was taken March 1, 1939, the Section of Fine Arts had purchased 539 murals and sculptures for the decoration of public buildings throughout the country. Scores of other commissions were in process, and new competitions were being planned. Owing to its splendid achievements, Congress has made the Section of Fine Arts a permanent branch of the Treasury Department and established the quota of 1 per cent of the cost of each Federal building as a mandatory amount for murals and sculptural decorations.

The response of the nation's artists to the Section's patronage has been remarkable. Its files, containing sketches and photographs of work submitted by the artists in competition, constitute probably the greatest library of contemporary art information in America. Nearly every artist of competence has sent his work to Washington for consideration. Many of them—most of the best ones—have been awarded commissions. On pages 80, 82 and 102 of this book may be seen reproductions of mural panels which George Biddle, Reginald Marsh and Henry Varnum Poor painted for Uncle Sam, the world's greatest art patron.

Are the murals great art? That we cannot now say, but one thing is certain. They are better than the murals the United States government purchased under the system that formerly prevailed. That system was efficient—as a refined racket. In a speech recently before the President's Cabinet, Edward Bruce described it neatly. It operated on the principle of *noblesse oblige:* you scratch my back; I'll scratch yours. The artists on the "in" with Washington, those who could talk suavely at state dinners, formed a sort of official club—almost a closed corporation. They passed around the plums, with the architects cooperating wholeheartedly. Six of them distributed commissions worth $2,714,299. Art was indeed a lucrative profession, if you knew the right people.

Measuring Bruce's department by comparative figures reveals an illuminating picture. The Supreme Court Building and the Archives Building in Washington are generally awarded the atrocity prize as far as their artistic worth inside and out is concerned. The decorations—moist-eyed debutantes parading as Greek goddesses and statues posing as the departing spirit of Law, of Justice—cost exactly $630,400, under the old system. That figure is $42,638 more than it cost under the new system to decorate 420 Federal buildings in widely scattered parts of the country.

Contained in Edward Bruce's speech before Messrs. Hull, Morgenthau and Hopkins were other passages that should be repeated here. "Mr. Mellon," he said, "paid $15,868,515 for 59 of the pictures which he has presented to his national gallery in his magnificent gift. The average cost of these pictures was $31,622 per square foot. The average cost of all the murals that have been executed by the Section of Fine Arts has been $14 per square foot. I do not say that our pictures are now worth Mr. Mellon's prices, but I do say, with absolute belief, that in the due process of time the government will find it has made a very good bargain and that these pictures will be valued at one hundredfold the prices which the government has paid for them. . . .

"I try to make our artists feel, and I think they do feel, that any one of them who receives a commission from us to do a mural in a post office has received a high honor which calls for the best they have to give. I tell them of a little village I know in Italy nestling in the Apennine Hills which is called Borgo San Sepolcro. In that village there is a little town hall no bigger than the average country post office. Also, in that village lived a great artist. His name was Piero Della Francesca, and he painted there the greatest picture in the world, *The Resurrection of Christ.* Whenever I am in Italy I make a pilgrimage to Borgo to see that picture, and I find my soul refreshed from seeing it, as do the thousands of pilgrims who visit it each year. I hope the day may come when we, too, may develop a Piero Della Francesca."

In the meantime Americans can view in their post offices, the courthouses and other public buildings paintings by some of the best artists contemporary America has to offer. They were placed there through an honest competitive system that is both flexible and fair. American art was thus brought before the eyes of millions of American people who daily pass through the buildings of their government. It is the world's largest art gallery.

While the Section of Fine Arts was developing, the burden of relief was assumed by the other arm of the government-in-art, the Federal Art Project, erected within the structure of the WPA in the spring of 1935. At its head was placed Holger Cahill, an art authority who had been trained in administration, museum work (under the late John Cotton Dana) and criticism. As an expert in the field of American folk art, he acquired a firm conviction—important in the whole Project pattern— that America has a great handicraft tradition.

Cahill set up the Federal Art Project as an all-embracing art activity in which the restrictions could in many cases be turned into advantages. With few exceptions, every artist on the Federal Art Project must be certified as in need of home relief before he can be enrolled. That is the major restriction.

Since the Project was not designed to operate with the leading American artists but with the least successful—good or bad—Cahill entertained little thought of hatching a brood of geniuses. Convinced of the importance of a backlog of artisan and handicraft tradition for any great national art, Cahill decided that if some of his employees were not good artists they could be good, honest artisans. He and his assistants then patterned the Federal Art Project as a regionally scattered agency for creating art, exhibiting art, teaching art, recording art and establishing art centers.

Cahill's goal is to conserve the talents and skills of artists who, through no fault of their own, find themselves on relief rolls and without means to continue their work, to integrate the fine with the practical arts and, more especially, the arts in general with the daily life of the community— these in brief are the primary objectives set forth by the WPA Federal Art Project.

What has been accomplished? What has been the cost? These are questions that call for statistics. A report dated April, 1939, states that the Project has executed and installed more than 1,300 murals in public institutions (on Page 104 may be seen a reproduction of the panel, *Controlled Medicine*, which William C. Palmer painted under Project auspices for the Queens General Hospital). The Project has produced 48,100 oil paintings and water colors, 3,562 sculptures, 84,000 prints, 850,000 posters—all for use by tax-supported institutions.

The Project has established more than a score of art centers in provincial areas, one of its most valuable accomplishments. It has circuited more than 500 art exhibitions, and more than 5,000,000 people have participated in its educational and exhibition activities. In New York City alone, 28,000 children and 8,000 adults are given the opportunity to express themselves in Project art classes. Through a division called the Index of American Design, Project artists have copied in water color rendering more than 10,000 facsimile reproductions of objects that are significant in the tradition of American handicrafts. These plates constitute one of the greatest source books of a national tradition in existence.

At its height the Project has employed approximately 5,000 needy artists. Of these, 46 per cent are engaged in creative work in the fine arts. The practical arts—posters, the Index, photographs, etc.—absorb 29 per cent. About 19 per cent are in the educational division, and about 6 per cent in the technical and coordinating categories. For this work, the government has expended on the Federal Art Project approximately $19,000,000 (about three-tenths of one per cent of the total amount spent on work relief). The Project, on its part, has adhered closely to its purpose of relieving needy artists and has spent 94 cents of every one of these dollars on labor.

From the above figures and facts it is obvious that the aims of the Federal Art Project and the Treasury Department's Section of Fine Arts are diametrically opposed. Yet in a certain sense they are complementary: the former concentrates upon a wide spreading of art activity; the latter specializes in procuring the peak achievements of the nation's finest artists, both famous and unrecognized, through anonymous merit competitions.

The benevolent attitude of the government toward art has had a profound effect upon art growth in America. The Project has been one of the chief means by which the narrow boundaries of art appreciation have been broken and original art introduced to the public. Its financial aid to young artists, emerging from art school into a depression-ridden nation, has made it possible for these youngsters, some destined for the top, to continue as artists. It has drawn the attention of the people to art as a national function, and has helped in the acceptance of the artist as a typical American, a necessary element in community life. Out of economic misfortune have come riches, for the government's entry into art patronage has started an era of incalculable wealth for the nation—both artistically and economically. Good art, like wheat, cotton, oil and washing machines, is worth banker's gold. Italy could wipe out her entire national debt by selling just a fraction of the product of great artists of her past.

More important to the future than the financial help the Project has extended to individual artists is its creation of a reservoir of art interest and activity throughout the nation, and particularly in those sections once artistically arid and despoiled by the migrations of artists to such metropolitan centers as New York's Greenwich Village. Thomas C. Parker, Deputy Director of the Federal Art Project, states that when the government entered art, 85 per cent of the artists were concentrated in only nine metropolitan centers. The Project has worked continually to check this cultural erosion by encouraging the artists in their home regions. And on the impulse thus given by the government other forms of art are flourishing and will continue to flourish, so deeply rooted are these in the national life—at Midwestern universities students paint pictures for their college degrees, in Midwestern towns such as Bloomington, Ill., merchants and bankers and townspeople organize exhibits of national art.

Has the Federal Art Project been worth its cost to the taxpayers? In its semiannual battles with Congress the Project has never been called upon to defend its cultural returns to the country. Its struggle has been to counteract the small but noisy minority of left-wing political agitators.

Let us focus our vision on the coming generations—after the good has been recognized and white-wash has done its damnedest for the rest—then, when time has softened the harsh edges of contemporary personalities, the decision, I believe, will be that the Project was worth every dollar it cost—and many more.

Is there an American art?

When this persistent question last arose in the summer of 1938, after critics in Paris and London had reviewed with disfavor the canvases of contemporary America, Jewell in the New York *Times* wrote words of memorable encouragement to America's doubters. His language was plain:

"Let it be stated at once, in plain, blunt language, that we have always had an American art and that we shall continue to have an American art . . . as long as America continues to be a racial entity in the brotherhood of nations. There need be no palaver of compromise, half-statement, or wistfulness here. Let it be advanced not tentatively, not timidly, not apologetically, but instead as a Categorical Imperative, that we have an American art."

How, then, explain the recurrent waves of foreign influence in American art? The *Times* critic answered this by distinguishing between modish copying and true assimilation—between *adoption* and *adaption.* "If the artist be truly an artist and make these great gifts [of past schools] his—part of his own experience—and if in turn the speech of his art be truly the utterance of his own vision, then, almost as if it were a miracle, the art that comes to us from him will seem irradiated with genius of place, of race, of time, of clime."

These were reassuring words to the multitudes of hypochondriacal American artists when they were printed a year ago. The firm conviction of this critic's words carried tremendous weight. Scores of American artists were encouraged and took his and Walt Whitman's advice "to sing what belongs to him or her and to none else."

There is an American art, and from the historical section of this book it may be seen that we have had isolated examples in the past. Copley was an American artist until he stopped being an American. Eloquent proof of the existence of an American art lies in the supreme difference between the canvases produced by the young Copley in Boston and those done by Copley the Englishman in London. After Copley there were American artists, the main difference between them and the American artists of today being their lone, sentinel-like existence. There were Homer, Ryder and Eakins, each a giant amid a paucity of real, native painters. These men in their time lacked the golden environment for a great, all-embracing American art. They lacked what today is a miraculous fact: a receptive public mood for a real American art.

Today the American people want an art that is their own. And there are artists who have found in the new conditions and the new demand a release that was denied their predecessors. The artist's wings are no longer clipped. He is required only to keep faith with the American spirit, for it is this alone that shall brand his art as American. For this alone is America's gift to her artists.

To describe or identify the American spirit in art or life is hazardous. But some of its manifestations are familiar, especially in contrast to the spirit of other nations.

America has none of the fine genius for hedonism that is part and parcel of every Frenchman. French art excels in charm and in the exquisiteness of its taste. Conformity is English. With the sons of Britain, tradition is sacred. Their genius is in literature, and their art has always been handmaiden to the story, the anecdote, the setting. The Dutch love life's substance, and Dutch art is an expression of their stolid concern for man's hard-won possessions. It is honest painting of things honestly acquired. The neighboring Germans, on the other hand, are given both in their art and in their national history to a tendency to overdramatize themselves, to sentimentalize.

Where in this pattern does America fit?

In American art there is strength, realism, sometimes fatalism. Because of our Anglo-Saxon heritage American art is a literal, three-dimensional art. There is little room in its pattern for such purely aesthetic detours as cubism or nonobjective painting. But because of the inroads of blood from the south and east of Europe we will never be content with the cold representationalism of the English. We demand warmth and something of substance beneath the canvas surface. Synonyms for the American spirit are easily found, but none so quickly suffices as the electric word: dynamism.

American artists are at peace with nothing. They roam over the vast theme of Man and his Environment. The two are protagonists in nearly every contemporary American painting, each jostling the other, working changes, adjustments and compensations. Man and his environment and the constant warfare between the two are in America's song, for out of that warfare the nation's painters subconsciously hope to find the New World Symphony.

Benton's most recent canvases are in this American spirit. Haunted by the jealous revenge of Dame Nature against the greediness of Midwestern farmers, he painted *Persephone* (Page 69), a Missouri allegory. The nude form of a Missouri girl, whom the artist would call a Greek Goddess, reclines with none of the charming ease and flowing softness of a European nude. Even while asleep she is tense, controlling the entire canvas with a nervous dynamism. The tense acrobats and circus girls of Walt Kuhn, painted in the simplest of terms, are quiet dynamos of human beings, eloquent of the brash role they perform in life—as American as any figures ever painted.

The solitary quiet of a Sunday, when man has declared a truce with his environment, is the time that Edward Hopper paints in his rows of houses or lonely lighthouses. In the full glare of a stark, uncompromising light he studies, with the fatalistic impersonality of a scientist, the things men have built. No charming Frenchman, no serene Dutchman could take Hopper's point of view. No one but an American.

With a range of color so frugal as to drive most French artists to despair, the native-born Charles Burchfield paints his drear November America, with its gingerbread architecture and ponderous steel structures. The air may be crisp and sharp; it may be dust-laden with heat, or moist with fog and damp. Whatever the weather in a Burchfield landscape, the darks and the lights and the values between vibrate with the precision of a tuning fork. That is dynamism.

The American spirit is to be felt in the racy robustness of Reginald Marsh's New York streets and theatres, turmoiling with humanity; the struggle of nature and the animal kingdom of John Steuart Curry's landscapes; the tense moodiness of the sea in a Henry Mattson marine; the *rigor mortis* of Grant Wood's relics of wiredrawn American physiognomy; the clever animation of dancing light on an Alexander Brook figure; the luscious color and strong, silent yearning of a Frederic Taubes composition.

There is no definite style of painting in American art. Some, like Curry's and Jon Corbino's, are Rubensesque. Grant Wood traces back to Colonial portraiture; Hopper to the Dutchman Vermeer; Kuhn to the sculpture of archaic Greece; Henry Lee McFee, Alexander Brook and a host of others to the modified modernism of Cézanne.

Style, it may be said, is one of the last infirmities of a national art, the first indication of national decadence. When style becomes an easily recognized national characteristic, sclerosis of the American spirit will have set in. But today the American painter's will is the wind's will. He may appropriate the oldest Italian aesthetic discovery, that of perspective, or he may steal the thunder of Bali's art. But whatever he takes, if the electrolysis of his own American spirit is brought to bear on these borrowings, they are automatically fused into the new product—an American painting with an American identity.

Indeed, the very multiplicity of America's borrowings, the confusion of styles today, is, in a sense, proof of the vitality of the nation's art. It forms a complex pattern, which for convenience may be divided arbitrarily into four divisions of approach. One major block of painters is essentially classic, seeking form primarily in its painting. Another is the precisionist, precise in its technique, making an appeal less to the tactile sense of the fingers than to the visual reality of the eye. A third division is lyric; a fourth dramatic.

With differing degrees of strength the following painters fall loosely into a category of classic form: Edward Hopper, Leon Kroll, Edward Bruce, Charles Sheeler (in his Bucks County Barn period), Eugene Speicher, Boardman Robinson, Umberto Romano, A. S. Baylinson, Walt Kuhn and Kenneth Hayes Miller. These artists are interested in form—three-dimensional form—which they catch through the play of light. Their work appeals to the sense of touch, whether they are painting nudes, apples, lighthouses or blacksmiths.

Among those interested more in the visual reality of eye appeal—spiritual brothers of Vermeer and the Italian primitives—are Peter Blume, Edna Reindel, Luigi Lucioni, Georgia O'Keeffe, Alexandre Hogue, Grant Wood, Jerry Bywaters and Niles Spencer. These care less for tone relationships and atmosphere. They are what may be termed precisionists. Their work is cold and crystalline; contours are sharper and bathed in a uniformly bright light. They get their power from effective pattern. These artists are generally, like Blume, uncompromising, factual even in their dreams.

Among the nation's many lyricists in paint may be mentioned such mystics as Hobson Pittman and Henry Mattson, and such others as John Carroll, John F. Carlson, Nicolai Cikovsky, Frederic Taubes, Bernard Karfiol, Morris Kantor, Georgina Klitgaard, John E. Thompson, John Folinsbee and B. J. O. Nordfeldt. These are the moody ones, the dreamers and the mystics. They work sometimes in pattern, but more often in terms of light, shadow and chiaroscuro. They use color and form for emotional rather than aesthetic reasons and obtain, like Kantor, a certain flute-like quality, or, like Taubes, a certain violin tremolo that is essentially evocative.

Thomas Benton is a dramatist, and so is John Steuart Curry. Among other members of this group may be listed Reginald Marsh, Lamar Dodd, Eugene Higgins, Rockwell Kent, Barse Miller, Paul Cadmus, Jon Corbino, William C. Palmer, Edward Laning and William Gropper. These artists are interested in the implications of action in their subjects. They dramatize what they see, put life into motion, whether they are social protesting like Gropper, or reporting the common people like Marsh, or satirizing like Benton, or merely transmuting the action in their personalities, like Corbino.

Within these loose limits most of the best living American painters are plying their trade, though many, like Alexander Brook and Francis Speight, are combinations of two or more. Their approach and style, compounded of whatever it is, has been fused in an art that is unmistakably

American—a new art by a new people that strives today toward a new order. Providing he *adapts*, and does not merely *adopt*, the American artist is free to go back to the Old Masters or to take advantage of the latest art discovery, even if it come from Patagonia. American artists have the same rights to the heritage of Leonardo and Rembrandt as any European artist. Qualitatively it is folly to speak now of contemporary American art in terms of the Italian Renaissance or the high point of Dutch Seventeenth-Century painting. But the highest hurdle of all has been passed; the true American spirit has found its way into the paint and canvas of today's pictures.

One of the most illuminating comments made by French art critics upon the occasion of the Jeu de Paume exhibition of American art last summer came from Francois Fosca. Noting that the American artists have succeeded only in the present century in breaking the ties of foreign influences, M. Fosca concludes that the results are not happy.

"Contemporary painting in the United States," he said, "leaves a deceiving impression: the impression of an art created by intelligent, hard-working people but completely lacking in artistic sensitivity. They produce an art which is radically artificial, the same way that artificial silk or wool are synthetic products."

With these words M. Fosca was unintentionally paying America its first great foreign tribute. Of course, America lacks the brand of artistic sensitivity that lies in a French painting or a French dinner! Were it otherwise, it would still speak in a Gallic tongue. Our painters are no longer strumming outworn melodies; they are searching the higher rhythms, the new dynamics. They are creating, at last and on a wide scale, an art in harmony with the American spirit, in tune with the American way of life. There is an American art, as American as corn pone and dude ranches.

To the Art Patron

No art has bloomed for long without a great art public to support it. There is a prosaic side to art, the bread-and-butter side. An artist as a human animal must eat in order to keep the soul in communication with the body. The traditional romance of the emaciated artist starving in the garret of some ivory tower is bunk. This isolation of the artist from his patron was graphically depicted in a cartoon which Art Young did many years ago, showing himself in conversation with a young painter whose exhibition he was attending. "All that I have accomplished in art I owe to the struggle for the necessities of life," proudly said the young painter. "That's one way of looking at it," agreed Young. "If the cost of living goes high enough you might live to be greater than Michelangelo."

Economists, though bewildered by the longevity of the Great Depression, concede that America is approaching its imperial period of world dominance; that, as Rome was the center of the Mediterranean world and later England the center of the Atlantic world, America, lying between the Atlantic and the Pacific, is the center of the modern world of trade. When nations have been greatly enriched, a period of glorification of art has ensued. Look at Greece, at Italy when she was the center of the medieval world. Look at the later golden ages of Spain, of Holland and of England. As always, art grew out of these political and commercial ebbs and floods, reflecting accurately the drift of taste, and mirroring the concentration of talent in certain nations. What form will the art glorification of America take? The answer lies in large measure with the American art patron.

In America in recent years concerted efforts have been made to educate the public's taste for fine original art. Museums have multiplied; art has been made a regular part of the college curriculum; the radio has been utilized; national magazines like *Life* have spread art before the vast army of laymen; the government has done a magnificent job of widening the scope of art participation. The result has been a tremendous growth in art appreciation, but the actual patronage is still a thin trickle of what it was twenty years ago. We have today thousands of art lovers, but only a pitiful few love it well enough to live with it. Why?

Having spent most of my life amid warring artistic isms, whispered arty platitudes and acres of plush gallery walls, I would advance the following as David Harum reasons why art and people today have not yet met on common ground:

1. Failure of the modern artist to paint enough pictures the layman can live with on any terms of intimacy. 2. The layman's fear of trusting his own taste when it comes to a question of art. 3. Failure of the art dealer to dispel gallery fear as he displays his wares. The sacred atmosphere makes the layman afraid to ask prices. 4. The insidious advice of interior decorators who advocate bare walls, for bare minds. 5. The competition of department-store color reproductions, framed and guaranteed to give the average person of taste artistic colic. 6. The depression.

Merit in art cannot be measured by any hard and fast yardstick—as is the case in the practical sciences. The variations of taste are too many, and the standards are too loosely defined. Sensitiveness of perception, feeling for beauty, an open mind toward both the accepted art forms and the new adventurous developments, these are the only guideposts. Do not be ashamed of your taste. When you buy a painting, go about it in much the same way you would the purchase of a fine radio or an automobile. If a certain painting appeals to you, buy it, take it home, live with it and do not stand in awe of the artistic opinion of your neighbor. Taste, after all, is a personal matter. I like modern furniture; maybe you do not. But that does not make either of us right or wrong. Art is a commodity that some creative spirit has produced to give you a more beautiful environment in which to live.

Liking is the first step toward true art appreciation. Art is meant to be liked and lived with. To buy an artist's work is the highest compliment you can pay his brush or his chisel. Try the time-tested process of trial and error. Acquire today what you like. Tomorrow, as you grow in artistic perception, you may discard and substitute. This is the system museums use in purchasing contemporary art, and it is what all great collectors have done even in the less risky field of Old Masters.

Of course, there is always the investment or gambling aspect to art collecting. This is incidental, but if your judgment or luck is good enough, you may repeat the experience of Fort Worth with Thomas Eakins' *Swimming Hole*. The Fort Worth Museum purchased the painting in 1925, only fourteen years ago and just nine years after Eakins died, from the artist's late widow. The purchase price was $700. This summer the *Swimming Hole* is on view in the "Life in America" exhibition at the Metropolitan Museum and the insurance value placed on it is $7,000. In fourteen years the Eakins picture increased 900 per cent in value. At the prevailing rate of compound interest in a New York savings bank, Fort Worth's $700 would now be about $800. But art paid Fort Worth 16½ per cent compound interest, and its $700 is $7,000.

Association with art and artists is the best avenue toward a correct estimate and comprehension of art. Beware of suitcase art dealers escorting in trailers nebulous Old Masters and vague references.

Annually innocent American art buyers pour thousands of dollars into the coffers of itinerant art dealers for faked or worthless paintings which are carted in trailers off the beaten track to be sold, at auction or privately, as "Gainsboroughs," "Corots," "Rembrandts," "Ryders," etc. These suave salesmen pander to the most popular of American weaknesses, the desire to get something for nothing. Buy your art either directly from the artist or from established and reputable art firms. If you patronize carpetbaggers who carry their "art" in trailers attached to automobiles, you will soon find that you have acquired nothing for something.

Also beware of over-ballyhooed foreign portrait painters, sporting heels polished by constant clicking. Patronize your local art exhibitions. Absorb in museums as you would in a great cathedral the indefinable sense of beauty that goes with things of the spirit. To know art, to have it about you in the home, make for the fuller life.

The reader will notice in these pages a conspicuous dearth of aesthetic evaluation, no flights of art criticism. That has been left to the critics and the aestheticists; it is not the province of the art reporter to dwell in those upper zones. I have tried to share the thrilling experience of living in an historic age, to record through facts the development of the new American School of Art, trace the causes behind it, and to describe its coming-of-age as it fulfills its social, economic and artistic functions. No age can evaluate its own cultural achievements. Time alone can judge our efforts, decide if our art is great or minor. But of one thing we can be certain. This new American art is our own—yours and mine. It is America speaking. Let us listen.

BIOGRAPHIES

GEORGE WESLEY BELLOWS
(Born 1882, Died 1925)

THIRTY YEARS AGO George Bellows shocked the public by his realistic pictures of drunks, prize fights, and lovers at night in city parks. Eight years later, in 1917, Bellows' painting *Stag at Sharkey's* (page 42) brought him fame. Thereafter such canvases as *The Parlor Critic* (1921), *The Law is Too Slow* (1923) and *The Drunk* (1924) added to his reputation, and he became one of the greatest leaders of the new group of realistic painters who depicted everyday American life.

Born of Yankee stock in Columbus, Ohio, Bellows came to New York in 1904, after graduating from Ohio State University. He studied under Robert Henri and later under Kenneth Hayes Miller and H. G. Maratta. He taught at the Art Students' League during 1910, 1918 and 1919, and also taught at the Chicago Art Institute in 1919.

An athlete himself, he spent much of his time at clubs and arenas where he found excellent models for his prize-fighting series of lithographs and drawings. His book illustrations are considered among his best works, outstanding among them his drawings for Donn Byrne's *The Wind Bloweth* and H. G. Wells' *Men Like Gods*.

Bellows never went to Europe, and spent most of his later years in Woodstock, where he had his home just across the road from Eugene Speicher. Twenty-five museums own Bellows' work, and he is represented in almost every important American collection.

The *Stag at Sharkey's* is Bellows' best known painting. He loved the prize ring for itself, believed it "the only instance in everyday life where the nude figure is displayed." It shows two heavyweights slamming it out at the Sharkey Athletic Club. The canvas, owned by the Cleveland Museum, was sent to the now famous American Art Exhibition in Paris in 1938.

THOMAS HART BENTON
(Born 1889)

AMERICA'S MOST ABUSED, most talked-of, and probably most dynamic painter of the American Scene today is Missouri's Thomas Hart Benton. In 1935 Benton, convinced that New York's studio painters were "an intellectually diseased lot, victims of sickly rationalizations, psychic inversions, and God-awful self-cultivations," retired to his home state of Missouri after a stormy career of twenty years in New York.

Benton's life story is, in essence, the story of American Art. Born in southwestern Missouri in the hill town of Neosho on the fringe of the Ozarks, Tom Benton was named after his great-uncle and Missouri's first senator, and was brought up in the legal tradition of Missouri's famous political family. His father, Colonel M. E. Benton, was a lawyer and politician of the old school who came from Tennessee (where he had fought with Forrest) to Missouri shortly after the Civil War. He arrived, Tom Benton says, "riding a horse and knocking the snakes out of his path with a long stick." The Colonel tried to make a lawyer of his first-born and took young Benton on many of his political junkets up and down the state. But these excursions only aroused a love for adventure and travel, and left Benton with a lasting impression of the Missouri countryside.

At seventeen, chafing at home ties, Benton got a job as surveyor's assistant in the zinc and lead district near Joplin. He gave that up to draw cartoons for the local paper. But his father, still intent on educating him, got him enrolled in a military school in Alton, Illinois. Benton remained there only for the football season, then left for Chicago to study at the Art Institute. Once there, he got his instructor to persuade the Colonel to send him to Paris. Of these years in Paris, where he was called "Le petit Balzac," Benton says: "A girl friend to take care of you and run you, a studio, some work, a lot of talk and an escape into the world of pretense and theory. I wallowed in every cockeyed ism that came along." But he soon came to the conclusion that he "was no good anywhere. In the company of such hardened internationalists as George Grosz, Wyndham Lewis, Epstein, Rivera, and that Stein woman, I was merely a roughneck with a talent for fighting, perhaps, but not for painting as it was cultivated in Paris." He then studied the old Italian masters, but after four years came back to the U.S. and spent the next six years in New York in a disheartening struggle to earn his living. He worked as a stevedore, tried book illustration and ceramics. He ran an art gallery, taught art, and designed sets for the Fox Film Company. He was greatly interested in prize fights and joined a gymnasium, but still imbued with his Paris training, did not make use of his New York experiences in his paintings. His pictures, which he now began to exhibit, were abstractions, symbols, and a strange hodge-podge of impressionism.

When America entered the World War the Navy put him to work as an architectural draftsman. "This was the most important event in my development as an artist," Benton says. "I was forced to observe the objective character of things—buildings, airplanes, dredges, and ships—things so interesting in themselves that I forgot my aesthetic drivelings and morbid self-concerns. I left once for all my little world of art for art's sake and entered into a world which, though always around me, I had not seen. That was the world of America. Furthermore, I was thrown among boys with whom I discovered bonds of sympathy, boys from the hinterlands of the South, and I got along with them. They were interested in what was going on, not in their own egos. I felt perfectly natural and at ease for the first time since the old days in Missouri."

After his release from the Navy, Benton held his first important exhibition, inspired by his direct experiences. Some of his pictures sold and he became an instructor at the Art Students' League. Having turned his back upon "precious" painting, he spent his summers at Martha's Vineyard drawing the natives, and there began a sixty-four-panel pictorial history of the U.S. He completed sixteen, exhibited them and from then on was known as a mural painter. In this field his influence has rivaled that of the Mexican Diego Rivera.

In 1922 he married an Italian girl, Rita Piacenza. Two years later he went back to Missouri to his father who was dying of cancer. There he became reacquainted with his father's friends, discovered that he understood these old Missourians, and realized that his place was with them there in Missouri. He spent the next ten years traveling in America, studying the mines and steel mills, the industrial centers of Pennsylvania and Ohio, and made countless trips through the Deep South and the Far West. He lived with the hillbillies in the Carolina mountains. He went down the Mississippi to New Orleans. From there he went across Texas, and back again and again through Arkansas and Missouri.

Eight years ago Benton was commissioned to paint "Contemporary America" on the walls of New York's New School for Social Research. The mural was completed in nine months, and Benton became the most talked-of painter in America. Radicals accused him of having no real political conscience. His choice of subject matter was criticized. He was accused of degrading America. Critics shouted: "Cheap nationalism," "Tabloid Art," and "Modernist effrontery." A year later the Whitney Museum of American Art commissioned him to paint a mural for its library walls, and the following year he painted a 200-feet long by 15-feet high mural for the State of Indiana's exhibit at the Century of Progress. This netted him $5,000. Then the Missouri Legislature voted him $16,000 for the Jefferson City mural. Immediately thereafter the Kansas City Art Institute made him director of painting, and he returned in triumph to his native state. While he painted the 45,000 square foot Missouri State Capitol mural, he left the doors open for all to come and criticize. This work he completed in a year, only to be accused of holding a great state up to nation-wide ridicule. Critics could not understand why, instead of imaginary heroes and idealized statesmen, he portrayed *Huck Finn and Nigger Jim* (page 70), the Jesse James' hold-ups, Frankie and Johnny, Boss Pendergast.

Now at the height of his career, Benton's easel pictures are priced from $900 to $12,000. Once engrossed in a project he works from twelve to fifteen hours a day. He has lectured and written a number of articles on politics and philosophy, and published a book, *An Artist in America*. And he is continuing his teaching in Kansas City. Within the past two years his technique has changed and for the first time he is concerned with problems of craftsmanship. His new works are studies in design, detail and texture.

T. P. and Jake (page 70) portrays the artist's twelve-year-old son, Thomas Piacenza Benton, with his shepherd dog, Jake, at Martha's Vineyard, Mass., where the Bentons have a summer home. *The Jealous Lover of Lone Green Valley* (page 68), painted in 1930, depicts a Missouri hillbilly who has just stabbed his sweetheart. Here Benton has not yet developed his interest in realistic detail and textures. *Pussy Cat and Roses* (page 70), one of a new series of still-lifes, breaks away from mere storytelling and is a good example of Benton's new interest in textures. *Persephone* (page 69), is the most ambitious of Benton's latest works. Here the mythological goddess of nature is a realistic Missouri girl about to be violated by a local farmer. This canvas is priced at $12,000.

GEORGE BIDDLE
(Born 1885)

GEORGE BIDDLE (of the Philadelphia Biddles) has painted the underprivileged poor in his murals for the Department of Justice Building in Washington, D.C.; has designed screens, rag rugs and tapestries; made a marquetry tip-top table in mahogany, ebony and satin-wood; baked terra cotta figures and bowls, and has done some sculpture and made many lithographs.

He is credited with having been one of those who suggested the Federal Art Program to President Roosevelt.

Biddle's early New England training was constantly at war with his natural creative instincts, and was possibly the cause for his two physical breakdowns, at sixteen, and again at twenty-three.

Born in Ardmore, Philadelphia, George Biddle went from Groton to Harvard, there received his A.B. and later his LL.D. degree. During these years he had no thought of becoming an artist. Following in the tradition of the famous Biddle family of lawyers, he passed his state bar examinations at twenty-six, and then at last determined to become a painter. For the following four years he studied in Paris, Philadelphia and Munich. He says: "I gobbled up museums, French impressionism, cubism, futurism, the Old Masters; I copied Velasquez in Madrid, and Rubens in Munich; I fell under the spell of Mary Cassatt's passion and integrity, and through her eyes I was influenced by Degas. I was desperately in earnest to overcome my late start."

Then came the World War, in which Biddle served two years. With the war over he was free again to paint, but he was already thirty-four and still a student. He turned again to France and Europe, but decided to escape to the tropics and spent two years in a native Polynesian village, the only white man for miles around. About this time he became interested in design, and came to have a horror of uncontrolled emotional or expressionistic painting. So for two years in Paris he experimented in stone and wood, modeled in clay. He cut block prints and made designs for marquetry, embroidery, stitch work and pottery.

Biddle considers these two years unhappy ones, says: "Slowly I began to feel how different from our own is the French or Paris mentality; and I realized how actually different in motivation and content is our own best American art. Most French art—indeed most European art—is fluent, detached, critical, aware of its artistry; while our best American art has always been sensitive, inhibited, romantic, passionate, naïve in its realism, and often not too critical—thank God, perhaps—of the problems of aesthetics." He returned to America in 1922.

Of the rising cry that American artists to create vitally must live in America, he says: "I for one would be deeply unhappy anywhere else. But this goes not to the essence. Of course an American, if he be one, will create best in terms of his America. But an artist . . . must probe and know his own depths and then he can express not only his America but the world's life which is in each one of us."

Biddle was first married in 1917. After a divorce from his second wife in 1930, he married the sculptor Hélène Sardeau with whom he now lives at Croton-on-Hudson. They have a son, Michael John. Biddle has just completed government murals for the New Brunswick, N.J., post office, and is writing an autobiography to be published this fall. He is represented in the collections of the Whitney Museum, the Denver Art Museum, and the Dallas Museum of Fine Arts.

Biddle painted frescoes for the Department of Justice Building in Washington, D.C., of which *Tenement* (page 102) is reproduced in this book. The quotation beneath the panel, "If we would guide by the light of reason we must let our minds be bold," is from Supreme Court Justice Brandeis. In the *Tenement* panel Biddle used his friend, Henry Varnum Poor, as model for the man sawing wood. In another panel of the Justice Department series Biddle shows the same family transported to a better life in the suburbs.

HENRY BILLINGS
(Born 1901)

APAINTER BORN IN A WELL-TO-DO FAMILY often has a harder time of it than his poorer brethren. If father, grandfather, and great-grandfather were physicians, lawyers, or business men and properly educated in the best of universities, then of course the son must not break that family tradition. And if there happens never to have been a painter in the family, so much the worse for the unfortunate son who happens to be born with the creative urge. This creative urge becomes an unheard-of thing, and there is a great clan horrified at the strange carryings-on of a beloved son.

There was something of all this in the early life of Henry Billings, son of Dr. John Sedgwick Billings and grandson of John Shaw Billings, famous bibliographer of medicine, designer of the Johns Hopkins Hospital, and first director of the New York Public Library. After only a few years of formal education that terminated when he was seventeen, in what he describes as "general confusion," the artist served a short apprenticeship in various architectural offices. But he soon left to study at the Art Students' League, a decision which he says was "an appalling choice from the family's point of view, inasmuch as I obviously had no talent."

At the League he studied with Boardman Robinson and Kenneth Hayes Miller on and off for about three years. Then, in 1921, he went to Woodstock. There at first he had a hard time of it, spending one winter alone in a small studio shack, living on $25 a month, and refusing to ask his family for more. There, for ten years as an art student, he absorbed and watched the influence of what is generically called modern French art. While learning the discipline of abstract painting he became deeply interested in the possibility of using machine forms as a basis for mural decorations, in keeping with the new developments in modern architecture.

At the same time he felt the need, he says, "of breaking our academic bondage to the still-life, the uninhabited landscape and the studio nude. This interest in subject matter, whether it results in studies of the American Scene or Surrealism, or what have you, is indicative of the feeling on the part of most painters that the easel picture must be recharged with vital content."

Billings gave his first one-man show in 1928, and three years later held another exhibition of decorative panels, the designs of which were based on machinery. Five of these panels were acquired by New York's Museum of Science and Industry. Later he was commissioned to paint murals for the Music Hall in Radio City, and these were followed by two mural commissions from the Treasury Department for post offices in Lake Placid, N.Y., and Medford, Mass.

For the Ford Building at the New York World's Fair he designed a 40-foot mobile mural, probably the only mural in the world in which actual parts of machinery revolve and move. Although his mural projects have taken a great part of his time, Billings is continuing easel painting. One of his earlier canvases is owned by the Whitney Museum of American Art. His *Arrest No. 2* (page 103) is witness to his keen interest in the social problems of his fellow men, and his awareness of the life about him.

GEORGE CALEB BINGHAM
(Born 1811, Died 1879)

JUST AS IN HIS LIVELY PICTURES of river boatmen, frontier riflemen, fishermen, fur traders, and election-day crowds Bingham was artist as well as politician and pioneer, so was his own life devoted to two careers.

Bingham's family moved from his Virginia birthplace when he was eight, to Howard County, Missouri. There four years later his father died and Bingham had to earn his living as an apprentice cabinet maker and cigar roller. But when he met Chester Harding, who had just come to the frontier to paint a portrait of the then aged Daniel Boone, Bingham saw no reason why he too should not become a painter. He donned a handsomely curled wig (at nineteen an attack of measles left him completely bald), painted portraits of his frontier neighbors and earned enough to travel. He went to St. Louis, Philadelphia, Washington, and, eventually, Düsseldorf, Germany, where he studied art for a while. He was, however, for the most part, self-taught.

Bingham loved Missouri, his neighbors and friends, and never lost touch with his home state. Recurrently wading into the politics of Missouri he was finally elected to the State Legislature in 1848. He became a captain in the U.S. Volunteer Reserves in 1861, was State Treasurer in 1862, and was defeated for Congress in 1866. In 1874 he was president of the Kansas City Board of Police Commissioners, and the following year Adjutant-General of Missouri. In the meantime he painted the portraits of his fellow Missourians, did a lengthy series of genre pictures of Missouri life, and married three times.

So admired was he by his contemporaries that many of his paintings were engraved and published as prints by the famed Paris house of Goupil et Cie. They were making copies of his lithograph of *The Verdict of the People* (page 19) during the Siege of Paris in 1871 when a Prussian shell blew up the establishment.

Bingham often used his painting for propaganda. Best known is his *Order No. 11*, also known as *Martial Law*, inspired in 1863 when Bingham was State Treasurer of Missouri. The Union troops on the border were commanded by Brigadier-General Thomas Ewing, lawyer and abolitionist from Ohio. To clear the Kansas-Missouri border of armed gangs infesting the territory, Ewing issued Order No. 11, declaring martial law and decreeing the complete evacuation within fifteen days of the population of the border counties. Homes were burned and pillaged. Many of the sufferers were friends of Bingham. He swore to make General Ewing "forever infamous."

After the war he painted a picture of the forced evacuation of a Missouri farmhouse. In 1879 when Thomas Ewing ran for Governor of Ohio, George Caleb Bingham had his picture, *Order No. 11* shown from town to town in that state. General Ewing was defeated.

With today's absorption in the American Scene, Bingham's painting, forgotten for more than fifty years, is of particular interest.

Bingham himself, as a politician, ran in many such elections as he depicts in his *The Verdict of the People*, a colorful and exuberant canvas that belongs to St. Louis' Mercantile Library Association. In the dramatic *Daniel Boone Escorting a Band of Pioneers into the Western Country* (page 18), Bingham depicts the courage of his contemporaries in marching their families into dangerous and unknown lands. The scene is Boone's trek to Kentucky through the Cumberland Gap in 1775.

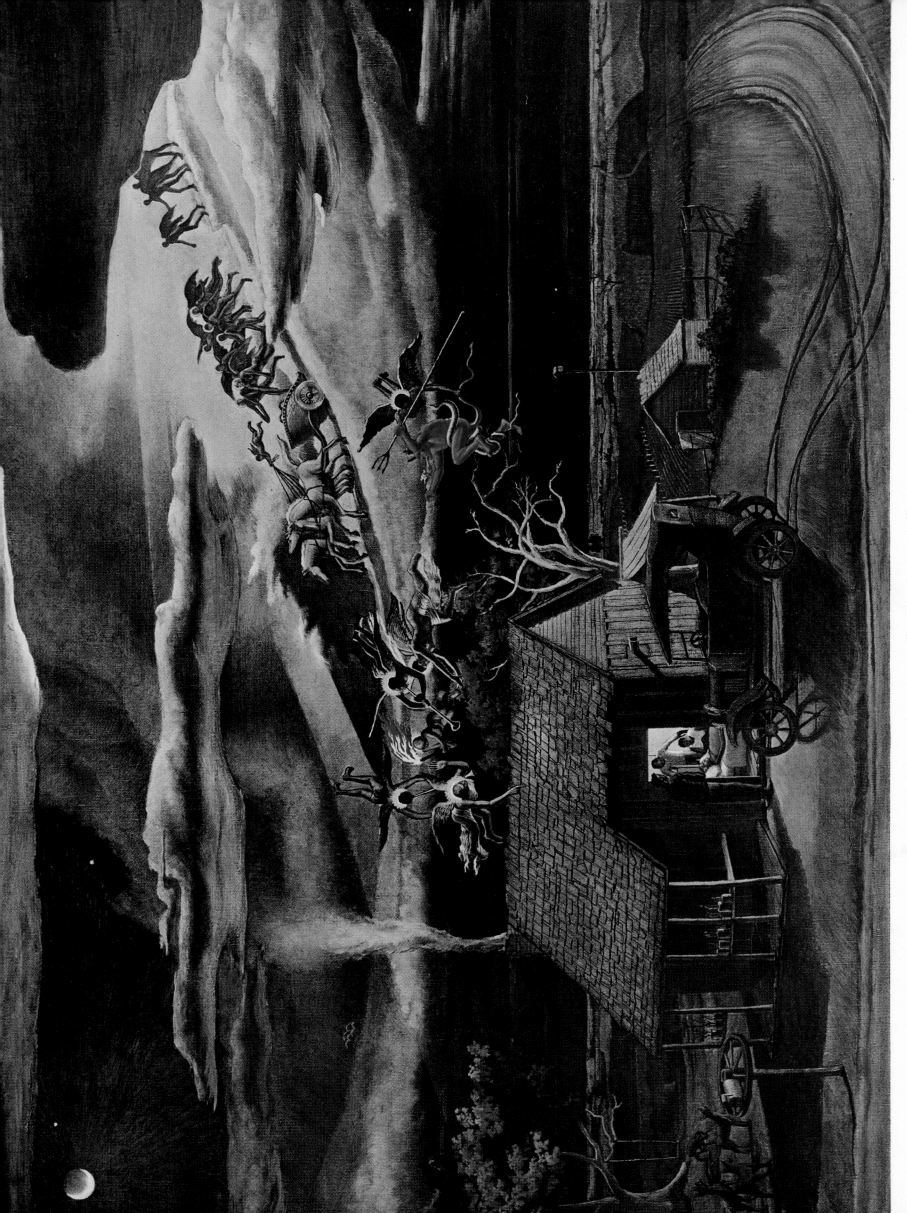

Swing Low, Sweet Chariot—JOHN McCRADY

Coney Island—PAUL CADMUS

Turtle Creek Valley—JOHN KANE

Vermont Classic—LUIGI LUCIONI

Tenement—GEORGE BIDDLE

Arrest No. 2—Henry Billings

*The Senate—*WILLIAM GROPPER

*Landscape Near Chicago—*AARON BOHROD

*Controlled Medicine—*WILLIAM C. PALMER

Doctor's Office—Raphael Soyer

Parade—PETER BLUME

ARNOLD BLANCH
(Born 1896)

WHILE PERFECTING A PERSONAL STYLE of painting Arnold Blanch developed a strong sense of social indignation, but though some of his recent canvases may be propaganda they are also art in the finest sense.

Blanch was born in the small town of Mantorville, Minnesota. There his mother painted on china and a maiden aunt gave drawing lessons. But Blanch did not think of a painting career until he was seventeen. He then enrolled at the Minneapolis School of Art for four years, where, under a German instructor, he learned something of the French moderns. With his fellow students, John Flanagan, Adolf Dehn, Harry Gottlieb and Lucile Lundquist (who later became his wife) he discovered *The Masses* with its drawings by Sloan, Bellows, Boardman Robinson and Stuart Davis. And through them he learned that an artist could find exhilarating material in the ordinary and the commonplace.

Blanch won a scholarship to the Art Students' League, and, with a $35 monthly allowance from his aunt, arrived in New York to paint and to live. He studied with John Sloan and Robert Henri.

He was drafted into the army during the World War, reached France a month before the Armistice. For the remainder of that year he traveled through the chateau country, and spent hours in the Louvre. Returning to America, he went home to Minneapolis, then again to New York to do posters.

Because he had had an attack of influenza while in the Army, Blanch was awarded rehabilitation compensation. With this he resumed his classes at the League, there studied under Kenneth Hayes Miller, and married his fellow student, Lucile Lundquist. They settled in Woodstock, conducted the Maverick cafeteria, wove and sold tapestries, and lived chiefly on the game Blanch shot. In 1926 Blanch held his first New York one-man show. Six pictures were sold, and two years later he went to Paris. Blanch held his second show in 1929 and the following year was appointed instructor at the California School of Fine Arts in San Francisco.

A Guggenheim Foundation Fellowship enabled him to travel again in Europe and this time he visited Belgium, France and Spain. Returning from Spain he went on the easel project for the WPA. Under the Treasury Department's Section of Fine Art he has completed murals for the Fredonia, New York, post office, and for the Norwalk, Connecticut, post office. In 1935 Blanch was appointed an instructor at the Art Students' League. He is one of the organizers of the American Artists' Congress. His pictures are owned by the Metropolitan Museum, Whitney Museum of American Art, and the Palace of the Legion of Honor in San Francisco.

Basket and Fruit (page 151) is a loosely organized composition, held together by the artist's harmony of color. Blanch received this fruit basket for Christmas, ate the fruit as he painted it.

PETER BLUME
(Born 1906)

BLUME'S METICULOUSLY PAINTED CANVASES have been labeled an "American form of surrealism."

Born in Russia, Blume was brought to Brooklyn when he was five and grew up there, attending evening art classes when he was twelve. While still in his teens, he tried to enter the National

Academy but was rejected. He was finally admitted to the beginners' class at the Educational Alliance, studied there while working at odd jobs in engraving and lithographing plants.

In 1924 Blume sold two water colors and decided to devote all his time to painting. He held his first one-man show in 1930. Two years later he won a Guggenheim Fellowship and traveled in Italy. He returned to settle in Gaylordsville, Conn., and in 1934 his canvas *South of Scranton* won first prize at the Carnegie International Exhibition, making Blume, then only twenty-eight years old, one of the most discussed painters in America.

Blume worked three years on *The Eternal City*, an anti-fascist polemic, depicting a Jack-in-the-box Mussolini amidst Roman ruins. He was able to complete this with the aid of his second Guggenheim award which he received in 1936. His canvases are owned by the Museum of Modern Art, and the Whitney Museum.

Parade (page 106) was given to the Museum of Modern Art by Mrs. John D. Rockefeller, Jr. With intense realistic technique Blume shows factories, billboards, rotary dust collectors and refrigerating plants giving birth to a suit of armor which is being paraded in triumph in the foreground of the canvas.

DAVID G. BLYTHE
(Born 1815, Died 1865)

WHEN PITTSBURGH WAS STILL A BACK-COUNTRY VILLAGE David G. Blythe, itinerant painter and writer of flowery verse, was born of Scottish immigrant parents in a forest clearing near East Liverpool, Ohio, just a few miles across the Pennsylvania line. He grew to be tall, lanky, red-headed, good-humored and eccentric.

Apprenticed to a Pittsburgh wood carver when he was sixteen, Blythe later enlisted in the Navy as ship's carpenter. When his enlistment was finished he returned home, set up as an itinerant portrait painter, made a steady living in those pre-camera days by painting likenesses of local characters at $15 to $20 per head.

Much of Blythe's verse was inspired by a pretty and popular home-town girl, Miss Julia Keffer, whom he married when he was thirty-two, and with whom he settled down over a store in Uniontown, Pa. There he was commissioned to carve a huge wooden statue of Lafayette for the new county courthouse. This caused the neighboring citizens of Waynesburg, Greene County, to want a similar monument to General Greene. Blythe demanded $300 from the Waynesburgers for the job. They retorted that they did "not propose to give him the whole county for his work," and hired a local craftsman. Blythe countered with a lengthy poem in the Uniontown newspaper, criticizing Waynesburg's clothes, public houses, manners, women and beds. Greene County had its own poet, too, who answered Blythe with angry verse. Blythe replied, describing Greene County as a "sow grown fat with buttermilk and meal."

And then misfortune overtook the eccentric painter. He painted an enormous panorama of western Pennsylvania landscapes and historical scenes. This he mounted on rollers and with it set out to tour the country, dreaming of making a fortune. But the project failed and he took to serious drinking. He settled in Pittsburgh and there began his paintings of the rough-and-tumble life of streets and taverns.

Blythe's lusty satires of loafers, pickpockets, drunks and bill collectors were displayed in the windows of J. J. Gillespie's art store, and "attracted such crowds that one could hardly get along the street." In return Gillespie gave Blythe a permanent drawing account, but he never took more than $5 at a time. During the Civil War he became a camp follower and painted several scenes of the war.

General Doubleday Crossing the Potomac (page 18) is a painting of a June day in 1863 when Union soldiers forded a shallow turn in the Potomac and marched over the green hills of Maryland. They did not know they were on their way to the great battle of Gettysburg. General Doubleday is credited with being the father of baseball, and the National Baseball Museum at Cooperstown, N. Y., was established in his honor.

AARON BOHROD
(Born 1907)

BOHROD FIRST BECAME KNOWN for his satires on Chicago. He was born on Chicago's West Side, the son of a Russian emigré grocer. He attended Crane High School in Chicago and spent one year at Crane Junior College. He began to study art at the Chicago Art Institute, and earned his way by selling score cards at the Chicago Cubs' ball park, as an advertising art apprentice, broker's clerk, and printer's paper-jogger. After a year at the Institute he left for New York to study under John Sloan at the Art Students' League. He says he learned a lot from Sloan "because he would criticize everybody's work in front of the whole class. And he knew what he was talking about." But he got little the second year from Kenneth Hayes Miller under whom he was studying lithography. Miller, he says, criticized by whispering in his ear, and he didn't like it.

Bohrod has twice won a Guggenheim Fellowship and has done a government mural for the Vandalia, Ill., post office. He is represented in the permanent collections of the Whitney Museum, the Art Institute of Chicago and the University of Illinois. In Chicago Bohrod is an active leader in radical movements.

When *Landscape near Chicago* (page 104) was first exhibited it raised a howl of protest from sensitive Chicagoans.

LOUIS BOUCHÉ
(Born 1896)

AN AMERICAN PAINTER of French ancestry, Bouché combines in his pictures the French tradition and the American spirit. And he is himself a rather rare combination—a good business man and a good painter. As a business man, and a very successful one, he is a member of the only firm of mural painters in the United States: Bouché, Saalburg & Henry, who will, for a good fee, decorate your home, your business office or a string of railroad coaches. The firm has just completed twelve panels for the bar lounge cars of the Pennsylvania Railroad.

As an easel painter Bouché is represented in an enviable number of American museums. He has painted government murals for the Department of Justice Building and the Department of Interior Building in Washington, D. C.

Louis Bouché can trace his art influence back to his grandfather, Ernest Bouché, who was a minor Barbizon painter and friend of Millet and Daubigny. His father, Henry Bouché, came to the United

States when he was sixteen and for a while designed jewelry for Tiffany's. Louis Bouché was born in Harlem, New York, and as a child spent as much time in France as he did in America. In 1915 the Bouché family settled in New York, and there Louis Bouché attended the Art Students' League, which he left after a year to open his own studio. With him went his fellow student, Alexander Brook, who is perhaps the only American who has influenced Bouché's painting.

Bouché was a sailor during the World War. After the war he was content to live for three or four years on the $25 a week his art dealer gave him in return for his pictures. Then in 1921 he married and his money-making career began when an art dealer hired him to become his gallery's stylist at $75 a week. He proved himself so excellent at organization and promotion that artists like George Biddle hired him to whip up publicity for them, and later Wanamaker's employed him to run their Gallery of Decorative Arts (the Belmaison Galleries, first modern picture gallery in a department store). In 1926 he left Wanamaker's to work for interior decorating firms, and made as much as $50,000 a year. At this time he also decorated the Radio City Music Hall Lounge. In 1930, when business began to fall off, he turned more to his easel painting, produced a number of abstractions that were not very well received by the critics. In 1933 he won a Guggenheim award and painted a series of landscapes.

His paintings are in the Duncan Phillips Memorial Gallery, Whitney Museum, Columbus (Ohio) Museum, and the Metropolitan Museum. The *Mural Assistant* (page 150) shows Bouché's brother-in-law sitting on a ladder.

ROBERT BRACKMAN
(Born 1898)

THERE WAS A FLURRY OF EXCITEMENT and curiosity in the art world last year when it became known that Robert Brackman had painted portraits of Colonel and Mrs. Lindbergh. The excitement soon died down but the curiosity has not been satisfied for the canvases have been exhibited only once in the United States in 1938 and at that time they were carefully guarded so that no photographs could be taken. It is said that they measure thirty by thirty-six inches and are framed in gray and gold.

The Lindbergh portraits marked a new high for Brackman, who had painted such other well-known people as Rabbi Stephen S. Wise, Helen Morgan (commissioned by Ziegfeld) and Mrs. Ellen C. duPont Meeds and her children.

Brackman was born in Odessa, Russia, came over to this country as a child, and grew up among radically-inclined people. He attended the Ferrer School where he studied economics under Emma Goldman and art under George Bellows. Later, while supporting himself by working nights as a photoengraver and lithographer, he studied at the National Academy of Design. In 1932 he was elected to the Academy and believes he is the only member of that organization who has ever held a card in the International Photo-Engravers' Union. Brackman has won many prizes for still-lifes and figure studies. He now teaches at the Art Students' League, lectures at the Brooklyn Institute of Arts and Sciences, and conducts his own summer classes at Mystic, Conn.

Brackman paintings are owned by the Metropolitan Museum, Newark Museum, High Museum, Addison Gallery, Brooklyn Museum and other public collections. *Arrangement, Life and Still Life* (page 149) shows Brackman's skill as a draftsman and colorist. The seated woman is Brackman's wife; the other figure is Ann Gutkin, famous Greenwich Village model. The painting is owned by the Delaware Art Center in Wilmington.

ANN BROCKMAN
(Born 1898)

ANN BROCKMAN'S PARENTS were so impressed with her drawing when she was only four years old that they covered a whole side of her room with a blackboard. On this blackboard she created a large family of characters, and with these she played as other children play with dolls.

Born in Alameda, California, Ann Brockman spent her childhood in Utah, Oregon and California, and much of it was an outdoor life on ranches. When she was seventeen, she married the artist William C. McNulty and with him came to New York to study at the Art Students' League. She sold the first magazine cover she made and says: "This was a terrific handicap—making money so easily almost spoiled my chances of ever being an artist." The artist's financial success in the advertising field continued and she sold many illustrations to *Collier's, Saturday Evening Post* and for advertising accounts.

In 1926 Ann Brockman returned to the League to study a month each under George Luks and John Sloan. Three years later she decided to give up all illustration and advertising work and has never returned to that field. She held her first show of her romantic paintings in 1930. For the past five summers she has conducted art classes at Rockport, Mass., in collaboration with her husband and Jon Corbino.

Nude (page 148) is heavily voluptuous in the Rubens style. The artist says she got the idea for this study when she went swimming with a young model in a secluded quarry near her summer home.

ALEXANDER BROOK
(Born 1898)

A "TEXTURIST" ABSORBED PRIMARILY IN PAINTING for the sake of painting, Brook differs from the professional portraitist in that he will not paint a subject that does not appeal to him. Therefore he accepts comparatively few portrait commissions. His attitude is best explained in his statement: "If I don't like it, I'll destroy it. If you don't like it, I'll keep it and sell it as a painting."

Born of Russian parents in Brooklyn, Brook's first real chance to study art came when he was twelve, after an illness of several months, when he was unable to walk. His instructor was a painter who made oil enlargements of family photographs. After entering the Art Students' League when he was seventeen, Brook discovered that he had much to unlearn, though his home work had given him a foundation for a successful career. He won a scholarship and spent four years at the League. In 1922, three years after he left the League, he began to exhibit his work. In 1931 he won a Guggenheim Fellowship, and that year the Whitney Museum published a monograph of his work. He is married to artist Peggy Bacon, and with their son and daughter they live at Cross River, New York.

He is represented in the permanent collections of the Brooklyn Museum, Metropolitan Museum of Art, Art Institute of Chicago, Whitney Museum of American Art, Albright Art Gallery, Gallery of Living Art, and many others. *Katharine Hepburn* (page 152) is a good example of contemporary American portraiture.

CHARLES EPHRAIM BURCHFIELD
(Born 1893)

CHARLES BURCHFIELD PAINTED THE AMERICAN SCENE long before it was officially labeled. He not only painted it but lived it, is still living it in a little white and green frame house with his wife, four daughters and a son in Gardenville, New York, a suburb of Buffalo.

Burchfield has never been to Europe. Most of his life has been spent around Lake Erie, and one of his ambitions is to be able to buy a farm and settle there.

Of Scotch-Irish descent, Burchfield was born in Ashtabula Harbor, Ohio. His father, a merchant tailor, died when Charles Burchfield was four years old, leaving the family penniless. Burchfield's mother encouraged him to attend the Cleveland School of Art for four years, where he paid part of his way by doing odd jobs. After art school he returned to his mother's home in Salem, Ohio, to work in an automobile parts company. There he married his neighbor, Bertha Kenreich.

Burchfield sketched and painted quick little water colors during lunch hours and every moment of his spare time. In 1916 he sold his first picture for $25. He continued his sketching and painting after his enlistment in the Camouflage Corps during the World War. In 1919 he returned to his old job in Salem and the following year had amassed enough good work to hold his first one-man show in New York City. Burchfield lost his job during the depression of 1921 and went to Buffalo where he found work designing wall paper. After eight years of this, painting only in his spare time, he finally decided to devote all his time to painting. Now one of America's most famous painters, his pictures are in the collections of the Metropolitan Museum, Newark Museum, Rhode Island School of Design, Boston Museum, Fogg Art Museum, Albright Art Gallery, Cleveland Museum, St. Louis City Art Museum, Detroit Institute of Arts, Nebraska University, Phillips Memorial Gallery, Museum of Modern Art, Whitney Museum of American Art, Brooklyn Museum, Syracuse Museum, Hackley Art Gallery, and other important public institutions.

In *Six O'Clock* (page 47) Burchfield depicts the end of a winter day in a suburb of identical homes. Notice how the yellow light from the snow-banked windows relieves the drabness of the scene and how the delicate crescent moon adds a touch of poetry. The last gleam of daylight over Burchfield's hometown, Gardenville, is dramatized in the painting *Over the Dam* (page 46). It is a scene a short distance from Buffalo Creek.

PAUL CADMUS
(Born 1904)

PAUL CADMUS SHOULD FOREVER BE GRATEFUL to the admirals of the U.S. Navy, for it was through the Navy that he, an unknown twenty-nine-year-old WPA artist, was catapulted to fame in 1933. They claimed that his picture, *The Fleet's In,* was vulgar, misleading, and gave the public "an erroneous idea of the behavior of the men." Admiral Hugh Rodman, U.S.N. retired, demanded that the painting be destroyed.

With stark realism that to some observers is "shocking," Cadmus paints that part of the American scene he knows best—New York City, Coney Island bathers, Greenwich Village cafeterias with young men flirting with each other, sailors misbehaving on Riverside Drive. He was born in New York City. His father was a painter, his mother an illustrator, and they began training him early in life to be an artist. Cadmus first studied at the National Academy of Design, then at the Art Students' League. When only seventeen he exhibited at the National Academy.

For three years he worked as commercial artist in an advertising agency, believes it gave him valuable training and discipline. From this he was able to save for a two-year trip to Europe. For five months he traveled from museum to museum, then settled on the island of Majorca, Spain, to paint. Returning in 1933, he went on the Federal Art Project for four months, painted *The Fleet's In* and one other canvas, *Greenwich Village Cafeteria.*

Cadmus says he is anxious to travel in America, especially through the West. He is represented in the Baltimore Museum. His *Coney Island* (page 100) is a brutal, detached recording of the masses at play.

JOHN CARROLL
(Born 1892)

JOHN CARROLL DOES NOT APPROVE of the Benton-Wood-Curry school of Midwestern realism, believing that it "gives us a view of American life through a knothole in a backhouse door." He says that if he were painting a picnic scene he "would like to idealize it instead of record the stark facts."

Best known for his emotional canvases of fluttering, fragile but passionate young girls, Carroll maintains that "imagination is one of the dominant and finest characteristics of the American people." Behind his art is the firm conviction that "people who live their lives among machinery like to escape from machinery." Tall, dark and pugilistic looking, he is in appearance the very antithesis of his pictures. He dresses like any average American, wears his hair cropped short, and lives on a 250-acre farm in Chatham, New York, where he raises cattle.

Carroll was born on a railroad train in Wichita, Kansas, as his parents were emigrating from West Virginia to California, where, later, he learned about cows and horses on his father's cattle ranch. He studied engineering at the University of California, left that to study art under Frank Duveneck in Cincinnati. "After six months," Carroll says, "I was sure I knew more about painting than Duveneck and he threw me out of his class."

During the World War he joined the Navy and drew portraits of sailors. In 1920 he settled in

Woodstock, and to earn a few dollars helped Bellows build his house and made frames for Eugene Speicher. He copied pictures in the Metropolitan Museum, sold them for whatever he could get, designed glass windows for Tiffany's, was at one time an elevator man, and even sold newspapers. Then in 1922 Carroll held his first one-man show. Two years later he was awarded the purchase prize by the Pennsylvania Academy for one of his canvases and went to Europe in 1925. He taught for one year at the Art Students' League, won a Guggenheim Fellowship later and again went to Europe. In 1930 Carroll was appointed head of the department of painting of the Society of Arts and Crafts in Detroit, and after he bought his farm in Chatham, New York, in 1934, he commuted each week during the winter to teach. In 1937 he painted a mural for the Detroit Institute of Arts.

Carroll is represented, among others, in the Detroit Institute, Los Angeles Art Museum, Pennsylvania Academy of Fine Arts and Toledo Museum. *White Lace* (page 154), femininely delicate in its pastel tones, is typical of Carroll's imaginative art, half ethereal, half sensual.

CHADWICK
(Active during 1850's)

AMERICA IN ITS EARLY DAYS had artists not only in its eastern centers of culture, but also among the pioneers—with those who blazed the trail westward, fought the Indians, and who explored the Far West. Most of these painters clung to a realistic style, depicting the everyday life of their fellows with scrupulous honesty and naturalism. Their paintings form the only pictorial record of a great part of the nation's history. When the Metropolitan Museum organized its exhibition, "Life in America," in the summer of 1939, the great wealth of this type of art was discovered and names long since forgotten in American art were revived and accorded respect. Chadwick, whose full name is not known, painted his account of placer mining in California.

Placer Mining (page 18), dated 1854, shows California "forty-niners" extracting gold from sand and gravel deposits by washing the latter in pans and troughs. The gold nuggets fell to the bottom as the gravel was washed away. The process is called "placer" mining, pronounced as though it were spelled "plasser." It depicts a period when any adventurer might find fortune in his shovel.

SAMUEL COLMAN
(Born 1832, Died 1920)

COLMAN WAS BORN IN PORTLAND, MAINE, and came to New York to study with Asher B. Durand. Later he studied in France and Spain, and became a member of the National Academy in 1862.

With the painting, *Emigrant Train* (page 18), Colman paid tribute to the pioneer spirit that dared push westward "the course of empire." The artist painted this picture in 1870, one year after the transcontinental railroad put an end to covered-wagon travel. Following the hazardous route of the Pony Express from Missouri to California, the Emigrant Train is fording Medicine Bow Creek in the Rocky Mountains near Laramie, Wyo.

JON CORBINO
(Born 1905)

CORBINO'S HEROIC AND TURBULENT COMPOSITIONS stem from Rubens and the reviving interest in Nineteenth Century French Romanticism.

Sicilian-born, grandson of a prosperous farmer and wine grower, Corbino was brought to New York City by his mother at the age of eight. They settled in the rowdier section of the East Side where Corbino's father joined them. Brought up in the midst of "gang wars" Corbino's early life was as turbulent as are his pictures today.

He studied at the Art Students' League, meanwhile earning his living as a soda fountain clerk, truckman's assistant and by making chocolates. During the summer of 1923 he earned his way through the Pennsylvania Academy's summer school by washing dishes. The following summers he worked in an apple orchard in New York State and as a farm hand in Connecticut. Greatly interested in animals, he once worked in a riding academy in Beacon, New York, made countless sketches and studies of horses. When only eighteen Corbino held his first one-man show in Ohio. Guggenheim Fellowships in 1936 and 1937 made it possible for him to devote his entire time to painting and sculpture.

Corbino has never returned to Europe, knows the Old Masters only through reproductions and originals in American galleries and museums. During the summer at Rockport, Mass., he conducts classes in painting for advanced students. He is represented in the following museums and collections: the Pennsylvania Academy, the Toledo Museum of Art, Addison Gallery of American Art, Sweet Briar College, Ball State Teachers College of Muncie, Indiana.

Flood Refugees (page 45) was painted in Rockport, Mass. Of this picture Corbino says: "I made many preliminary studies and drawings, and although the material rendered may not have any direct resemblance to the locality, much of the material I work out from local color."

RALSTON CRAWFORD
(Born 1906)

OF HIS GEOMETRICALLY PRECISE SCENES of man-made landscapes, Ralston Crawford says: "While I have no desire to reduce painting to a series of cog-wheels, I believe that the machine—mass production—plays a very important part in modern aesthetics." His paintings of grain elevators, mills, smoke stacks and lonely highways are, he feels, "distinctly of the time—they offer a new visual stimulus which is considerably more relevant than the wooded dell." He cannot, he insists, "think of this period as one in which a school of nature poetry will bloom."

Born in Ontario, Canada, Crawford came to the United States when he was four, went to high school in Buffalo, later became a sailor and landed in Los Angeles where he studied at the Otis Art Institute and worked in Walt Disney's studio in 1927. After studying at the Pennsylvania Academy, at the Barnes Foundation for two years, and the Breckenridge School in Gloucester, he spent three years in Paris. Returning to America, he settled in Chadds Ford, Pennsylvania, where he now lives and paints.

Crawford held his first New York one-man show last March, and the Whitney Museum owns one of his canvases. *Overseas Highway* (page 126), showing a stretch of the new 170-mile Florida-Key West Highway, is an example of Crawford's belief that artists should utilize machine age designs.

JOHN STEUART CURRY
(Born 1897)

PAINTER OF RURAL AMERICAN LIFE, and particularly of Kansas, Curry is the youngest member of the famed Benton-Wood-Curry trio, regional painters of the American Scene. It is fitting that Curry has returned to the Middle West to live and paint at the University of Wisconsin as Artist-in-Residence in its College of Agriculture. Descendant of many generations of farmers, he was born in the hamlet of Dunavant, Kansas. His family, originally from Scotland, emigrated to South Carolina and later followed the line of the frontier into the Mississippi Valley.

First-born of five children, John Steuart Curry says: "I was raised on hard work and the shorter catechism. Up at four o'clock the year round, doing half a day's work before we rode to town on horseback to our lessons."

His mother gave him his first glimpse of the Old Masters through reproductions she had collected on her honeymoon. He was sensitive to all natural phenomena even as a child and on the farm drew pictures of animals, windstorms and catastrophes of the plains about him, and they are to this day his favorite subjects.

Never of a studious nature, he broke away from the country high school in Winchester, spent that summer as a railroad section-hand, was able to buy himself a suit of clothes and left for Kansas City to enroll at the Art Institute. A month later he moved on to the Art Institute of Chicago, remained there for two years, supporting himself by sweeping floors and acting as bus boy in the school's cafeteria.

Upon America's declaration of war, Curry went to a training camp, only to be sent home when it was discovered that he was still under age. In 1918 he enrolled at Geneva College, played football for two seasons and spent the following five years trying to earn his living as an illustrator of blood-and-thunder scenes for popular western story magazines. He married and then persuaded art patron Seward Prosser to loan him $1,000. With this he spent one year in Paris at laborious study. He returned to America penniless, settled in Westport, Conn., swore that he would turn out a worthwhile picture or give up painting entirely. There in 1928 from memory he painted his first famous picture *Baptism in Kansas* (page 73). Gertrude Vanderbilt Whitney bought it for her museum and subsidized him for two years at $50 a week.

Again from memory in 1930 he painted *Tornado over Kansas* (page 71). Three years later it won second prize at the Carnegie International Exhibit. His wife died and he gave up his studio in Westport, secluded himself in a drab New York studio. He taught at Cooper Union and the Art Students' League, and held a show of circus studies after touring New England with Ringling Bros.-Barnum & Bailey Circus. Curry painted *Circus Elephants* (page 72) in 1932. The circus people liked Curry but quibbled over minor technical errors in his series of circus pictures.

In 1934 he married Kathleen Shepard, returned to Westport, recovered his old enthusiasm and painted *Line Storm* (page 72), considered one of his finest western landscapes. Westport, beginning to appreciate him, commissioned him to do a double mural for the local high school. The United States Government selected him to paint murals for the Department of Justice and the Department of Interior Buildings in Washington, D. C. He was appointed Artist-in-Residence in the College of Agriculture, University of Wisconsin, in 1936. At $4,000 a year he has his studio on the campus, mingles with the students but conducts no formal classes.

Curry urges community appreciation of art; once remarked that "it would be a lively and fitting thing if a community which had raised a well-bred and excellent herd of cattle or a prize-winning horse, or developed an unusual food product, could have these celebrated in good paintings on the walls of community buildings."

Of government sponsorship of art Curry says: "The public has been startled into liking or dis-liking it, and for the first time realized that painting was something that could exist outside a museum. I believe that the present administration's program of sponsoring painting, sculpture, music and the drama is of tremendous importance to the American art of the present and of the future. . . . In our youth . . . art as a reality was as foreign as a Chinaman. Within these few years there has been an absolute revolution in the symbol and subject matter of American painting. . . ."

Kansas, long neglecting its native son, has recently commissioned Curry to do a series of murals for its Kansas state capitol in Topeka, for $20,000. His paintings, comparatively few in number, are owned by the Metropolitan Museum, Whitney Museum, Michigan's Hackley Art Gallery, University of Nebraska, St. Louis Museum, and other public institutions and private collectors.

Tornado over Kansas represents man's elemental terror of nature, expressed in the artist's own boy-hood fears and emotions. A tornado in 1931 skirted the Curry farm. Two years before, Curry painted the violent scene, in which a Kansas tornado is seen swirling on a rural home in the form of a terrible horn of destruction. As in many a Curry work, a great deal of life is organized into a compact composition, dominated in this case by the tornado funnel and the big, red-headed Yankee father, shouting at his distracted sons, while his green-faced wife enters the cyclone cellar. *Line Storm* (1934), which was owned by the late Sidney Howard, shows a thunderstorm breaking over the rolling Kansas farmland, where every hill gives a 20-mile view. The hay is loaded and the mules have started for the barn, down the hill across the road, as the first lightning zigzags across the sky.

GLADYS ROCKMORE DAVIS
(Born 1901)

GLADYS ROCKMORE DAVIS' RECENT QUICK RISE TO FAME has been almost phenomenal. She is one of many artists like Marsh, Ann Brockman and Sloan, who first made their way by commercial art work. Until a few years ago, Gladys Davis was known only as a fashion and advertising artist.

She was born in New York City and at sixteen enrolled at the Chicago Art Institute where she studied for three years. In 1925 she married the noted illustrator, Floyd Davis. They now have two children, a son and a daughter. She spent 1932 in Cannes, France. There, with her husband, Gladys Davis painted and decided to devote her entire time to fine art. Returning from Europe, she studied at the Art Students' League, and with George Grosz for a year.

The artist now lives in New York during the winter and spends her summers at Barnegat Bay. Gladys Davis captures in her paintings a verve and lilt that have earned her unusually rapid acclaim.

The first picture she submitted to a national show won a major prize. She paints such scenes as *The Pink Skirt* (page 148) without a model, believing that in this way she gets more spontaneity in her work.

THOMAS EAKINS
(Born 1844, Died 1916)

IT WAS IN THE ERA OF THE NOT SO GAY NINETIES that Thomas Eakins was fired from the Pennsylvania Academy because he insisted on teaching drawing from nude models. Eakins had taught at the Academy for ten years, but was never popular during his lifetime. As an instructor, his criticisms were considered too frank, and his paintings were judged too realistic for the sentimental age in which he lived. Appreciation, however, has grown rapidly in the last decade, and today Eakins is one of only three American artists to be accepted by the Louvre.

A descendant of Scotch, Irish, Dutch and English pioneers, Eakins was born in Philadelphia and there died at the age of seventy-two. When he was twenty-two he went to Paris, but soon left for Spain where he was influenced by the works of Velasquez and Ribera. Returning to Philadelphia in 1870 he opened a studio, hoping to find fame and fortune as a portrait painter. But Eakins attracted few commissions. He was a poor showman and his brush told too much of the truth. He did, however, receive a commission from the Union League Club to paint a portrait of President Hayes.

Arriving in Washington, Eakins was told that the President had no time for sittings. Eakins insisted that he did not need special sittings, persuaded the President to permit him to set up his easel in the President's office and paint while Hayes worked. It was summer and the President worked in shirtsleeves. Eakins saw nothing incongruous in painting his subject just as he was. The Union Leaguers, however, found the painting "absolutely scandalous," and promptly rejected it. After much haggling the portrait was paid for, but never hung. It disappeared and to this day has never been found.

Sargent, to his lasting credit, was one of the few contemporaries of Eakins who recognized his worth. On a visit to Philadelphia, he was asked if there was anyone in particular whom he would like to meet socially. He promptly asked to see Eakins. Sargent's friends admitted they had never heard of him, and Sargent had to spell out the painter's name so that they could locate him in the city directory. They could have asked Walt Whitman, had they known where he lived.

While painting, Eakins was particular that his models resume the same pose day after day. To insure this he stood them against a background marked out with squared lines and attached colored ribbons at the exact point where elbow, knee, head, etc., were to be.

Toward the end of his life Eakins began to receive public recognition. At the Columbian Exposition of 1893 he was accorded a medal, and the Paris Exposition of 1900 gave him an honorable mention. Gold medals were awarded him by the Pan-American Exposition of 1901 and the St. Louis Exposition of 1904. The National Academy of Design elected him to full membership in 1902. In 1910 Eakins became ill, never painted again and died six years later. In 1930 his widow gave sixty of his paintings to the Pennsylvania Museum of Art as a memorial.

The works of Eakins, the realist, and Ryder, the romanticist, are often linked. Eakins' biographer, Lloyd Goodrich, says: "While most of their generation were pursuing shadows, these two had in common the fact that the worlds they created, different as they were, possessed depth and substance. The dream world of Ryder was as real as the naturalistic world of Eakins. Their minds, directed in the one case outward, in the other inward, were the most profound in the American painting of the last generation."

Max Schmitt in a Single Scull (page 22), portrays Eakins' boyhood friend, an athlete and oarsman, in his racing shell "Josie" on the Schuylkill River at Philadelphia just above the Girard Avenue Bridge. To sign his picture, Eakins included in the work a miniature portrait of himself in a scull rowing at good speed and in excellent form. On the stern of his boat appears his name, Eakins, and the date. Eakins painted this picture in 1871, not long after his return from Europe.

STEPHEN ETNIER
(Born 1903)

ETNIER'S EARLY LIFE was a series of rebellions. He wanted to be an artist but because he happened to be born the son of a wealthy turbine manufacturer, he was expected to carry on his father's business. At Yale (class of 1926) he failed in his studies and then transferred to the Yale Art School. However, the stilted academic training was not to his liking, and he soon left. At this point Etnier persuaded his father to let him take up painting as a career, and he set up a studio in Philadelphia. Later he studied with Rockwell Kent and John Carroll.

At Gilbert Head, Popham, Maine, where he and his writer wife, Elizabeth Jay, live and own several hundred acres of an island, Etnier has recently painted a series of romantic and imaginative landscapes. Of painting in general he says: "A successful painting is a contrivance for pleasurable escape designed to be looked at not in a museum or gallery, but in a home. . . ."

Etnier held his first one-man show in New York in 1930, and since then his pictures have been bought by the Metropolitan Museum, Phillips Memorial Gallery and the Wadsworth Athenaeum. Living by the sea, Etnier spends a great deal of time in a boat. The sailor who helps him with the boat is often used as a model. This sailor was the first model for his painting *Adolescence* (page 130). But Etnier changed his mind, dismissed the sailor model and got his wife to pose. The scene is outside the Etnier home at Gilbert Head, Maine.

JERRY FARNSWORTH
(Born 1895)

OF HIS OWN WORK Jerry Farnsworth says: "I don't believe in labels. I myself don't know where I belong, with what group of painters. The Academy hangs my painting, and Homer Saint-Gaudens invites it to Pittsburgh. I believe every artist should be an individualist, appreciative of the giants of the past and interested the while in every new manifestation which presents itself."

Farnsworth has many supporters in his belief that "America is surely marching forward to new goals since its break-away from the French School, and not even the artists themselves yet realize what great work may result in the not too distant future." He started as a "Sunday painter," and now feels that "portrait painting is more fun than any other phase of art. The continuous parade of interesting people make it a most exciting profession." The artist's father was a storekeeper in the small town of Dalton, Georgia, when Jerry Farnsworth was born. There had never been another artist in the family and he showed no indication of becoming a painter until he was twenty. As a child, after the early death of his father, he spent a wandering life through the South. When he was sixteen his family moved to New York City, where his mother found work as a trained nurse.

In 1916 Farnsworth enlisted in the Navy and, while stationed in Washington, attended the Corcoran School of Art at night. After the World War he continued his studies, and in 1921 went to Provincetown to paint with Charles W. Hawthorne. When he was twenty-seven Farnsworth decided to devote all his time to painting. Now, with his artist wife, Helen Alton Sawyer, he lives in Provincetown during the summer and in Scarsdale, New York, in the winter. In 1933 he became an associate member of the National Academy of Design.

His pictures are in the collections of the Delgado Museum, Pennsylvania Academy of Fine Arts, Museum of Fine Arts, Houston, Texas, and the Vanderpoel Art Association.

The Dancer (page 148) is a study of a model who lived near the artist's home at Cape Cod. Contrast Farnsworth's technique with Ann Brockman's painting of this same model on page 148.

VAUGHN FLANNERY
(Born 1898)

FLANNERY'S LIFE IS EQUALLY DIVIDED between art and the breeding of horses. When he travels abroad he goes to look at two things: paintings by Titian, El Greco and Tintoretto, and the horse races in France and England. And in his pictures are the love of fine textures and emotional painting plus the excitement of the race track. He is a director of the Maryland Jockey Club and breeds horses at Cockade Farms, Darlington, Maryland, where, at intervals, he takes time off from his work in a New York business office to paint.

Flannery is of American native stock. His father's family (they were in the old packet trade on the Ohio and Mississippi in the pre-Mark Twain days) settled in Kentucky in 1836. His mother, a painter, came from the family of Kents who were painters, designers, and craftsmen back to William Kent of England for whom Vaughn Flannery has named his son. The Kents settled in Carolina before the Revolution.

While he was recuperating from diphtheria as a child, Flannery's mother gave him her pastels and paints to keep him busy. He has been making pictures, he says, ever since.

The Flannery family moved to Chicago when he was still a child, and there he attended Saturday classes at the Art Institute. His mother wanted him to study painting, his father urged architecture. Vaughn Flannery later attended the University of Illinois, and during the World War trained for the Camouflage Corps. After the war he married Didy Ettinger, the Philadelphia painter, traveled in Spain, and returned to settle in Maryland. Of his divided career of fine art and business, Flannery says: "I have had to figure out my own way of taking care of myself. Nobody asked me to paint and as long as my present situation is left undisturbed, I have no kick coming."

One of his paintings is owned by the Phillips Memorial Gallery in Washington, D. C. *The Maryland Hunt* (page 130), somewhat romantic in feeling and color, is filled with the exciting action that holds the artist to his second love, horse racing.

LAUREN FORD
(Born 1891)

LAUREN FORD'S IMAGINATIVE PICTURES have about them a dreamlike quality that shows nature not quite as it is but as it should be; or, perhaps, as you might like it to be. Her pictures frequently include children and often have a religious theme.

Artist-farmer, Miss Ford lives the year round on a farm in Connecticut. Many of her paintings are of her farm and the neighboring countryside. She began learning to draw when only eighteen months old because her mother had decided Lauren was to become an artist. Later, she studied at the Art Students' League, New York City. Because she is an uncommonly modest person and has never been dependent upon her art for a living, she did not exhibit her pictures until 1928. After her first show in New York City her pictures were eagerly bought, appreciated not only by wealthy urban collectors but by her farmer neighbors and friends. Many of them have the salty sense of humor she inherited from her lawyer father, the late Simeon Ford, famous after-dinner speaker and part owner of the Grand Union Hotel in New York.

Her grandparents moved from Indiana to Connecticut about eighty years ago. Of Connecticut she says: "I guess it's in my blood." She spends as little time as possible in cities, takes occasional trips to the south of France. Lauren Ford pictures are owned by the Metropolitan Museum, Corcoran Gallery of Art and the Art Institute of Chicago.

The Country Doctor (page 78) depicts the Connecticut countryside where the artist lives and owns a farm. Note that each little section might well make a separate painting, and that this canvas is the composite product of any number of individual sketches made by the artist at different times.

EDWIN FULWIDER
(Born 1913)

FULWIDER, YOUNG INDIANA PAINTER, is interested in "Americans at work, industrial scenes, farm and country scenes, but always figures—Americans at work." His principal aim, he says, is "to bring to everyone the thrill I get from a train or an airplane, or a quiet scene, a crowd, or some historical fact or event that has a direct bearing on our everyday life."

A star pupil of the John Herron Art School in Indianapolis, Indiana, he studied there for five and one-half years, receiving a Bachelor of Fine Arts Degree. After completing the regular course of training, Fulwider was awarded a scholarship for travel and study in the eastern United States, and on that jaunt he visited all the principal schools, museums, and private art collections. Returning to John Herron for another year, he graduated in 1936 and was awarded the Milliken traveling scholarship for travel and study abroad, and spent the following year in England, Holland, Belgium, France, Switzerland and Italy.

He is a native Hoosier, born and raised in Bloomington, Indiana. At present, with his wife and son, he is living in Nashville, twenty miles from his home town, where he devotes himself entirely to painting and lithography. He says: "I take all my subject matter right from life." *Dead Head* (page 76) is one of those increasingly popular "action" pictures, showing an engine and caboose running without a payload.

EMIL GANSO
(Born 1895)

A JOVIAL, SANDY-HAIRED GERMAN shuffled into the art gallery of Erhard Weyhe in New York City fifteen years ago and said: "I am a baker. And my name is Emil Ganso." With him he had a portfolio of drawings which, he explained, he had done during his spare time. The pictures were not good enough to exhibit, but Weyhe was impressed with them, signed Ganso to a long contract, and gave him a small weekly allowance on which to live and continue to paint.

A frankly sensuous poet in paint, Ganso is of mixed German, Spanish and French ancestry. Born in Halberstadt, Germany, he began to draw almost before he could talk. Forced to earn his living from early childhood, he became a baker, and continued that trade when he came to the United States in 1912. He attended the National Academy of Design for a few weeks and later became a friend and pupil of Jules Pascin.

Ganso is as well known for his etchings, lithographs and aquatints as for his paintings. In 1933 he won a Guggenheim Fellowship. His works are in the following collections: Worcester Art Museum, Addison Gallery of Art, Boston Museum, Los Angeles Museum, Whitney Museum of American Art, Denver Art Museum, Metropolitan Museum, Detroit Institute of Arts, Cleveland Art Museum.

In *Bearsville Meadows* (page 128) Ganso depicts the Woodstock country where he has spent six months annually for the past fifteen years. With oil and water-color he has painted this valley in every season and in all its moods.

WILLIAM GROPPER
(Born 1897)

AN ARDENT COMMUNIST SYMPATHIZER, William Gropper is still probably better known for his propaganda cartoons than for his painting, although his recent exhibitions have been well received by the critics, and museums have been buying his paintings. Today he ranks with the top few of America's Social Protest artists.

Born on New York City's lower East Side, Gropper at fourteen was already working in a sweatshop, twelve hours a day, six days a week, for $6 weekly. He worked there steadily for four and a half years, studying art at night. Later he washed dishes in a Second Avenue beanery and continued his art studies. He studied at the National Academy of Design and at the New York School of Fine and Applied Arts.

Gropper did not become actively "class-conscious" until he became a cartoonist for the *Tribune* in 1919. Sent with a reporter to cover a feature story on the I.W.W., he resigned from the *Tribune* to work for the *Rebel Worker*, the I.W.W. paper. Since then his cartoons have appeared in the *New Masses* and in many national papers and magazines.

In 1927, with Theodore Dreiser and Sinclair Lewis, he went to Moscow as a guest of the Conference on Cultural Relations of Soviet Russia, later published his book, *Sketches of Soviet Russia*.

Gropper's first exhibition of paintings in 1936 was a surprise to everyone who knew him. He had been painting quietly, without showing his work, for fifteen years. Gropper refuses to compromise

House by the Railroad—EDWARD HOPPER

Light House at Two Lights—EDWARD HOPPER

White Barn—GEORGIA O'KEEFFE

The Big Water—FREDERICK J. WAUGH

City Interior—CHARLES SHEELER

Overseas Highway—RALSTON CRAWFORD

Night and the Sea—Henry Mattson

View of Kingston—GEORGINA KLITGAARD

Bearsville Meadows—EMIL GANSO

Old Smuggler's Cove—JONAS LIE

The Maryland Hunt—Vaughn Flannery

Adolescence—Stephen Etnier

his social ideals for his career. In 1934 he was commissioned to paint a mural for the Schenley Liquor Corporation in which he caricatured Grover Whalen, who was Chairman of the Board of Directors, and Harold Jacobi, President. These jabs at capitalism were later erased.

Gropper painted another mural in 1936 on the Treasury Relief Art Project for the Freeport, Long Island, post office. The following year he won a Guggenheim Fellowship and made studies of the Dust Bowl. He is now working on a mural for the Department of the Interior, Washington, D.C. He owns his home at Croton-on-Hudson, New York, where he lives with his wife and two sons the year around.

His pictures are owned by the Metropolitan Museum, Whitney Museum of American Art, Museum of Modern Art, Hartford Museum, and the Museum of Western Art in Moscow, Russia. *The Senate* (page 104), one of Gropper's most successful works and one of the best of modern satirical paintings, is owned by the Museum of Modern Art.

ALEXANDRE HOGUE
(Born 1898)

HOGUE, LIKE SO MANY OTHER AMERICAN ARTISTS, discovered that he could paint best that which he knew intimately as part of his personal life.

As a boy Hogue worked on a cattle ranch in the Texas Panhandle, watched "suitcase" farmers (akin to present day "suitcase" art dealers) pour into the fine grazing lands, plow up grass roots on land never broken before, and plant corn and wheat for the temporarily lucrative boom market. He often heard old ranchers say: "If you plow up this land, it will blow away." In time he saw these prophecies come true. There were years of drought, then came the dust storms. In his paintings of the Dust Bowl he has shown the despair, the stifling heat, and the tragedy of Texas farmers. His *Drouth Survivors* shows two dead steers and a tractor buried in dust, and in *Dust Bowl* the hot sultry sun burns down upon a desolate dust-smothered landscape.

Alexandre Hogue, born in Memphis, Missouri, first came to know Texas when his father, a Presbyterian minister, settled there when the future artist was six years old. For a time he studied at the Minneapolis Art Institute, in 1921 arrived in New York. After four years of "hanging around New York art galleries," he decided that his best chance to enjoy life as well as paint life was back home in Texas.

Hogue has been teaching art to young Texans since 1925. He is represented in the Dallas Museum of Fine Arts. He painted a ten-panel mural in collaboration with Jerry Bywaters for the Municipal Building in Dallas.

Of such sadly familiar scenes as *Drouth-Stricken Area* (page 75), Hogue says: "These paintings of mine delve into mind reality by the use of symbols arranged in a perfectly logical way, so that the observer feels that he has actually experienced the scene. The trail and the greatest grazing land in the world have been destroyed first by the fence, then by over plowing and now by the drouth. . . . This is something else besides surrealism, and I would like to have it called 'psychoreality' since it plays on the conscious mind, not the dream world, and uses visual psychology to present the realities of the mind in an orderly fashion."

WINSLOW HOMER
(Born 1836, Died 1910)

IN A MOVABLE EIGHT-BY-TEN STUDIO that protected him from the cold nor'easters of the Maine coast, Winslow Homer for twenty-six years studied and painted the ocean with an understanding and intense love of the stormy waters that were a part of his Yankee inheritance.

Homer was born in Boston in 1836, the son of a wealthy hardware merchant. With his father's approval he went to work at nineteen for Buffard, a Boston lithographer. But he had little formal art training, attended only a few classes at the Academy of Design in New York and took a few lessons from Frederick Rondel, a French painter. *Harper's Weekly* commissioned him as artist-correspondent when he was twenty-three years old to cover Lincoln's inauguration and later the Civil War. His realistic drawings brought his name before the public, and for seventeen years he worked enthusiastically for *Harper's.* Later he used many of his Civil War sketches for his paintings.

When he was thirty-one and still working for *Harper's,* Homer took a ten months' vacation to visit France, but was little influenced by Europe. His first serious attempts at oil paintings were war subjects and American country life. Leaving *Harper's* he went to Petersburg, Virginia, to study and paint the negroes there. In 1881 Homer went again to Europe, this time spent two summers on the English seacoast at Tynemouth. There his interest in the sea was first aroused. Returning to America, now aged forty, he retired to Prout's Neck, Maine, at that time a hamlet of isolated fishermen's shacks. Taking over his brother's barn, he turned it into a kitchen-living-room-studio, and lived the simple life of a recluse. He raised his own vegetables, even his tobacco, and cooked his own meals. Homer had by then turned completely from the quiet rural scenes of his earlier work to paint realistic storms and shipwrecks. Most of his moonlight scenes were painted actually in the light of the moon, in his portable studio.

A small, slender, stiffly erect man with strong features and brusque New England humor, Homer spent the remaining twenty-six years of his life at Prout's Neck, with only an occasional trip to Florida and the West Indies, painting with reverent realism and native spirit his version of the American Scene.

Homer was a "special correspondent from the front" for *Harper's Weekly* when he made the sketches for his painting *Prisoners from the Front* (page 24). He painted the canvas, however, after the War, using his notebook of sketches for reference. The painting shows three Confederate prisoners being questioned by a Union officer. Homer painted *The Gulf Stream* (page 24) in 1899, twenty-three years after he had retired to Prout's Neck. This painting may have been inspired by Conrad's *Nigger of the Narcissus,* published in 1897.

EDWARD HOPPER
(Born 1882)

IN EDWARD HOPPER WE HAVE STARK PURITAN-AMERICAN REALISM. He paints the American scene practically devoid of life, carries the doctrine of simplicity to the extreme limit.

He had the good luck to be the son of sympathetic and intellectual parents who allowed him to develop his artistic bent naturally. Born in Nyack, New York, of Dutch-English ancestors who had lived in America for generations, Hopper first studied at the Chase School under Robert Henri and Kenneth Hayes Miller, with a group of fellow students that included Guy Pène du Bois, Rockwell Kent, George Bellows, Glenn Coleman and Gifford Beal. Hopper came to know the Impressionists after five years at the Chase School when he went to Paris in 1906 for a year. He earned money for this trip with magazine illustrations and spent the year painting the streets and architecture of Paris.

Hopper exhibited these Parisian street scenes in the "First Independent Show" in March, 1908. Exhibiting with him were other Henri pupils, including Coleman, Bellows, Kent and du Bois. Hopper's painting passed almost unnoticed. The year of the Armory Show, 1913, was a turning point in American art history and was also an important year for Edward Hopper. Oddly enough, at the Armory exhibition, which introduced modern European art to America, Hopper, acknowledged today as one of America's most American painters, sold his first canvas. But he was scarcely heard from again until his one-man exhibition at the Whitney Studio Club in 1919. The next important event in his career, four years later, was the sale of a water color to the Brooklyn Museum. This was the second picture he had sold in twenty-three years. His water-color show in 1924, however, was a complete success. Hopper then turned to oils and was accepted in important national exhibitions.

Although today he is paid from $1,500 to $3,000 for a canvas, he is far from wealthy. A painstaking, careful worker he turns out only a few paintings a year. For the past twenty-five years he has painted and lived in a simple studio-and-bedroom apartment on Washington Square.

Writing on America's debt to French art, Hopper says: "If an apprenticeship to a master has been necessary, I think we have served it."

His pictures are in some of England's principal museums and in the collections of the Metropolitan Museum, Whitney Museum of American Art, Brooklyn Museum, Boston Museum, Chicago Art Institute, Fogg Museum, Cleveland Museum, to mention but a few. *Light House at Two Lights* (page 124), is a public favorite, always in demand for exhibitions. The scene is at Cape Elizabeth, Maine, painted in 1929. Owned by Mrs. Samuel A. Tucker of New York, it is so often borrowed for exhibitions that she says it is "like having a very pretty debutante daughter. It is never at home." Hopper describes *House by the Railroad* (page 123), painted in 1925, as an impression of many such homes he had seen, with an air of faded glory . . . before the railway came. It represents a house of the President Grant era.

PETER HURD
(Born 1904)

PETER HURD'S FATHER SPENT CONSIDERABLE TIME and money trying to turn a naturally gifted artist into a soldier. After graduating from the New Mexico Military Institute (where he was chief bugler, and drew cartoons for the cadet publications), young Hurd was shipped off to West Point. But he spent so much time sketching and painting that he flunked math in his second year and was dropped.

Next, young Hurd was sent to Haverford College in Pennsylvania, where he met the noted mural painter and illustrator, N. C. Wyeth, who was so impressed with his talent that he took him on as an apprentice. In his spare time Hurd attended the Pennsylvania Academy of the Fine Arts. So convinced was Wyeth of Hurd's genuine talent that he persuaded the father to let his son give up college and devote his entire time to painting. Hurd in 1929 married his sponsor's daughter, Henriette Wyeth, who is herself an accomplished painter. They have two children, Peter and Ann Carol. Their studios are on Hurd's ranch in San Patricio, New Mexico, not many miles from his birthplace, Roswell.

Hurd takes his ranching seriously. To help improve it he trades pictures for building materials and labor. Once he gave a local carpenter a dozen lithographs in payment of a bill; and at another time he traded a painting for a brood mare. Hurd augments his income by raising polo ponies.

Hurd has painted murals for the New Mexico Military Institute; for the post office at Big Springs, Texas (a Treasury Department commission); and for the post office annex at Dallas, Texas, also a Federal project. One of his paintings was recently purchased by the Metropolitan Museum, and he is also represented in the Art Institute of Chicago and the Wilmington, Delaware, Art Center.

Boy from the Plains (page 76) is a portrait of Earl Wagner, son of Hurd's crop tenant. Hurd said he painted Earl because his skin was richly sun-tanned and his clothes "interestingly time-worn and sun-faded." *The Dry River* (page 77) was painted near Hurd's ranch in New Mexico.

GEORGE INNESS
(Born 1825, Died 1894)

WITH A CANNY EYE TO THE FUTURE, George Inness' Scotch father was determined to make a grocer of his son. So young Inness at the age of fourteen was given a store all his own, completely outfitted, on the corner of Washington and New Streets in Newark, New Jersey. The son was as determined as the father to have his own way; when customers came to the store, the young proprietor hid until they left. And when he was alone in the store he painted.

Convinced that his son would never make a good grocer, the elder Inness consented to drawing lessons. When he was sixteen young Inness worked for a while with map makers in New York, and studied with a French landscape painter. When he was twenty he opened his own studio, became interested in the Hudson River School of painting. But two years later he felt the need to travel abroad, left for Italy to paint the scenery about Rome, and became deeply interested in the Old Masters. In 1854, Inness lived in the Latin Quarter of Paris, where he was somewhat influenced by the Barbizon School. Five years later he settled for a while in Boston and then in Medfield, Mass., only to return in 1871 to Rome to spend about four years.

In 1878, George Inness established his famous studio in Montclair, New Jersey, where he spent most of his remaining years, a productive existence that was ended by his last trip abroad to Scotland. It was in Scotland that the greatest of America's early landscape painters died at the Bridge of Allan on August 3, 1894. Last and most talented of the so-called Hudson River School, Inness added deeper color and simplified design to the misty romanticism of Cole, Durand and their imitators.

Peace and Plenty (pages 20-21), one of the star attractions at the recent Metropolitan Museum exhibition of early American Art, was painted in 1865 as a thankful offering for the end of the Civil War.

EASTMAN JOHNSON
(Born 1824, Died 1906)

EASTMAN JOHNSON WAS RESPONSIBLE for the accuracy of George Washington's uniform in Emanuel Leutze's famous picture of *George Washington Crossing the Delaware*, which now hangs in the Metropolitan Museum. While the picture was being painted in Düsseldorf, Johnson was Leutze's student. Leutze had his young pupil write to his father in America for an accurate description.

Johnson was born in Lovell, Maine. After his father, Philip C. Johnson, entered politics the family moved to Washington, D. C., and there, in the Senate committee rooms, Eastman Johnson made many crayon portraits of such celebrities as the widow of Alexander Hamilton, the famous Dolly Madison (she was then an eighty-year-old lady), John Quincy Adams and Daniel Webster. With this he earned enough to finance a trip to Dusseldorf. After traveling extensively in Europe, Johnson settled for a time at The Hague, and there did so many portraits of his friends that he was called "the American Rembrandt."

Returning to the United States in 1855, Johnson was one of the first to paint the American Indian. Three years later he settled in New York, and in 1860 he was made a member of the National Academy. For the rest of his life he worked long hours in his top-floor studio on West 55th Street. His favorite subjects were New England rustics and negroes. He liked to paint his humorous characters wearing respectable old top silk hats at jaunty or pathetic angles.

Old Kentucky Home (page 19) is an idealization of slavery and illustrates romantic painting of America in the 1850's. This canvas belongs to the New York Public Library.

JOHN KANE
(Born 1860, Died 1934)

"I WANT TO PAINT PICTURES just as God made them," Kane once told his friends, and he wanted to paint Pittsburgh because the smoking, hilly city was his very own: one which he had helped to build.

A pious Catholic, born and reared in Scotland, Kane's real name was Cain, but a bank teller in Akron misspelled it, and the artist let it remain "Kane." "It makes no difference," he said, "as long as the money is safe." As a child in Scotland, young Kane attended school until he was eight and then, with the death of his father, went into the coal mines. Ten years later he was in America working as a "gandy dancer," tamping down the rocks between railroad ties. His next job was in a steel mill, but the enforced Sunday work, interfering with Kane's churchgoing, impelled him to quit.

During his long life Kane worked at dozens of jobs as a laborer and, while a railroad watchman, rescued a drunken cousin from a locomotive, lost one of his legs. His first painting job, in 1900, was an assignment to paint the sides of freight cars, and during lunch hours he amused fellow workers by making ad lib drawings on the cars.

This crude form of picture making held a fascination for Kane, and he launched into a side business of tinting photographs which often netted him as much as $15 apiece. In 1905 Kane began house painting, which was to occupy most of his remaining lifetime as a vocation while Sunday painting of Pittsburgh became his consuming avocation. Kane lived across from the Heinz pickle works in Pittsburgh, in the "Strip" section of the city, and this he painted feverishly during every spare moment. Each brick and stone, each chimney, mill and street car was scrupulously depicted in his honest canvases.

Not until he was sixty-five did Kane have the temerity to submit a picture to an exhibition. In that year, 1925, he sent a work to the famous Carnegie International Exhibition in Pittsburgh. It was promptly rejected by the jury. The next year he again submitted and was again rejected. The third time, in 1927, he met with success and the Carnegie International proudly exhibited a work by the newly discovered Pittsburgh "primitive." Two years later Kane's picture won a prize in the same show. One of the earliest private collectors to buy Kane's work was Mrs. John D. Rockefeller, Jr., and success slowly began to come his way. He gave up house painting for easel painting but never became prosperous, and in 1934 died of long-neglected tuberculosis.

Turtle Creek Valley (page 101), a Pittsburgh scene, is scrupulously honest in vision and in painting. Every little detail, the tiniest distant window, is given a place in Kane's peaceful, pious world.

GEORGINA KLITGAARD
(Born 1893)

A LYRICAL "TEXTURIST" in her sensitive handling of paint, Georgina Klitgaard is chiefly interested in the changing seasons and moods of landscape in the neighborhood of Woodstock, New York. She is also a skilled portraitist of family life and growing children.

Georgina Klitgaard was born and educated in New York City, studied for a short time at the National Academy of Design. In 1933 she traveled in Europe on a Guggenheim Fellowship, later painted a mural for the Goshen, New York, post office, and is now working on a mural for Poughkeepsie. She has lived in Woodstock for the past seventeen years.

Her pictures are in the collections of the Brooklyn Museum, the Metropolitan Museum, the Dayton Art Institute, and the Whitney Museum. In *View of Kingston* (page 128), she has caught the peace and spirit of a quiet Hudson River town.

LEON KROLL
(Born 1884)

LEON KROLL HAS BEEN A PERSISTENT PRIZE WINNER in the important national and international exhibitions since 1912. Two years before winning his initial prize, he held his first exhibition of paintings and sold his first picture for $100. That show was the beginning of a brilliant career and brought him many friends, among them Speicher, Glackens, Henri and Bellows. But it was Winslow Homer who had, earlier in his career, urged Kroll to paint.

Born in New York of impoverished, music-loving parents, Kroll has had to earn his own way since he was fifteen. As a child he used to haunt the old red brick and granite Metropolitan Museum. He worked his way through the Art Students' League by sweeping floors and washing brushes. His first teacher was John H. Twachtman. Later he studied at the National Academy and in Paris.

Kroll has been teaching painting since 1911 in leading American art schools, among them the National Academy, the Art Students' League, Mills College, Chicago Art Institute, Maryland Institute of Art, and the Pennsylvania Academy. Since 1913 he has been included in the Carnegie

International shows. His work hangs in twenty-one museums and public institutions, and he has painted murals for the new Justice Building in Washington, D. C. Kroll is now working on a large mural commission for the Worcester, Mass., War Memorial Hall, a project that he expects will take him three years to complete.

Figure Outdoors (page 151) is typical of Kroll's sensitive landscapes, in which he skillfully includes a figure for composition.

YASUO KUNIYOSHI
(Born 1893)

KUNIYOSHI IS A PAINTER of New York sophistication and is one of America's finest "texturists." Though he has been in this country for thirty-three years, he is not permitted to become a citizen because of his Japanese birth. And though his pictures are in many leading American museums, the Metropolitan is not permitted to buy his work from their fund for contemporary American art because of his "alien" status.

Kuniyoshi was born in Okayama, Japan. While still in his teens he set out to see the world and landed in Los Angeles. There, with children half his age, he went to school, drew apples and cubes so well that his art instructor advised him to become an artist.

From Los Angeles Kuniyoshi journeyed to the studio of Kenneth Hayes Miller in New York, earning his way as dishwasher, grape picker and ranch hand. He says: "I have done nearly everything but commercial art. But it is not true when they say I worked as a butler." He also studied at the National Academy of Design and at the Art Students' League.

In 1919 Kuniyoshi married the painter Katherine Schmidt (since divorced), and later studied abroad in France, England, Italy and Spain. In 1931 he returned to Japan for a visit and in 1935 traveled in Mexico on a Guggenheim award. He now spends his summers in Woodstock.

Kuniyoshi is represented in the permanent collections of the Whitney Museum, Museum of Modern Art, Columbus (Ohio) Museum, Brooklyn Museum, Albright Gallery, and the Chicago Art Institute. Kuniyoshi is best known for his sensuous female figures, beautifully wrought backgrounds and such unusual assemblages as *Objects on Sofa* (page 150).

RICHARD LAHEY
(Born 1893)

RICHARD LAHEY ONCE SAID: "I believe art should be enjoyed by the artist as well as by the public. It should not be a deadly serious thing, so sophisticated and grim as to frighten off the average layman." And in the work of this popular painter and art instructor there is combined with realism the essence of living. He believes that "nearly every artist, consciously or unconsciously, incorporates in his work definite traits of personality that reveal his real self in an intimate way."

As principal and teacher at the Corcoran School of Art in Washington, D. C., and Professor of Fine Arts at Goucher College, Md., Lahey has molded the artistic lives of thousands of art students. Previous to his appointment at the Corcoran School in 1935, he taught for twelve years at the Art Students' League. Of his students he says: "I come to admire them more and more—their intelligence, spirit, strength and fine character." He is convinced that "American art right now is in the healthiest and most vital condition it has ever been. Independent, adventurous, with strong fresh breezes blowing in it."

Lahey was born in Jersey City, and first studied at the Art Students' League as a pupil of Robert Henri and George Bridgman. After four years at the League he did free-lance drawing for the old New York *World Magazine*, drawing human interest subjects about New York City, and people of the theater for Alexander Woollcott who was then theater critic for the New York *Times*.

He served for eighteen months in the U. S. Naval Reserve during the World War and in the Camouflage Corps, and thus first saw Paris. After the War he painted steadily for six months and held his first exhibition. This resulted in an invitation to teach at the Minneapolis School of Art. "I felt," he says, "after the first week that I had said all I ever knew and would have nothing left for further criticism, but I have been going ever since." While teaching at the League he met and married Alma Carlotta Gonzales, then a sculpture student.

Lahey's work is in the collections of the Whitney Museum, Brooklyn Museum, Metropolitan Museum, Toledo Museum, Pennsylvania Academy, Addison Gallery of American Art, Detroit Institute of Arts, New York Public Library, and the Newark Public Library. He also has a government mural in the post office at Brownsville, Pa. His canvas, *My Wife* (page 150), is an excellent example of his sensitive portraiture. Mrs. Lahey posed for this picture three hours at a time, thirty-three times. It was a notable canvas in the great exhibition of contemporary American painting which Roland J. McKinney arranged for San Francisco's Golden Gate Exposition.

EDWARD LANING
(Born 1906)

ABRAHAM LINCOLN SPLIT RAILS for Laning's great-grandfather, who loaned Lincoln the money to go to Springfield when he was elected to the State Legislature. That was in Petersburg, Illinois, and there Laning was born. His mother's grave lies just across the path from that of Anne Rutledge in the little town.

Concerned with America and painting American life, Laning's dream is "to start out across the country in a car with canvas, paints, and brushes, and go to the first county seat I come to. There I'd ask the local citizens if I could paint them a mural in the courthouse—something that really depicted their community, its history or its place in American life today. I'd do this for the cost of the materials and my support while at work, plus just enough to get on to the next town. By the time I'd have reached the West Coast I would have made some beginning in building up an art really related to our life."

While still a high school student in Petersburg, Laning spent two summers at the Art Institute of Chicago. Later he attended the University of Chicago for two years, then studied at the Art Students' League in New York. After a trip to Europe in 1929 he returned to the League to study with Kenneth Hayes Miller, whose influence he had been resisting up to that time. When Miller took a year's leave of absence, Laning replaced him as instructor at the League.

Laning wanted desperately to be a mural painter but having no walls to paint, did five large mural panels on his own. The exhibition of these in 1933 led to a commission for a fresco for the

Hudson Guild Settlement House in New York. Following that he worked for two years on a mural for the Aliens' Dining Room at Ellis Island—a WPA commission and he is now painting a series of murals for the New York Public Library (5th Avenue and 42nd Street). He also painted a mural for the Rockingham, N. C., post office. The Whitney Museum owns one of his paintings. In 1939 he painted *T. R. in Panama*, first of *Life's* commissioned paintings. *The Corn Dance* (page 74) depicts Santo Domingo Indians of New Mexico performing strange rites to make corn grow. In the foreground tourists carry on still stranger antics.

DORIS EMRICK LEE
(Born 1905)

IN DORIS LEE'S EXUBERANTLY PEOPLED CANVASES of bucolic life are expressed the self-confidence and gaiety of a painter who enjoys life.

Born in Aledo, Illinois, the daughter of a merchant-banker, Doris Lee was the fourth in a family of six children. Her parents regarded her tomboyishness with misgiving. They did not, however, object to her drawing, and she recalls that her grandmother used to whittle and carve in wood. Her great-grandfather had retired from farming to paint.

She was educated at Lake Forest, Illinois, and Rockford College, where she was a student instructor in fine arts, and majored in philosophy. Upon graduation she married Russell Werner Lee, a chemical engineer from Ottawa, Illinois. They went to Paris for five months and there she studied with André L'Hôte. Returning, she continued her art study in Kansas City under Ernest Lawson, and at the San Francisco School of Fine Arts under Arnold Blanch.

In 1931 Doris Lee settled in Woodstock and has since divided her time between her studio there and New York's Fourteenth Street. Her paintings are in the collections of the Metropolitan Museum, the Art Institute of Chicago and the Rhode Island School of Design. She has painted a mural for the new Washington, D. C., post office. It was Doris Lee's *Thanksgiving Dinner*, winner of the Logan prize at the Chicago Art Institute, that started Mrs. Frank G. Logan, wealthy Chicago art patron on her crusade for "Sanity in Art."

The lunch hour love idyl, entitled *Noon* (page 48), was inspired by various Woodstock farm scenes. Before painting a picture, Doris Lee makes many quick pencil sketches which she later uses as notes in working out paintings like this one.

JONAS LIE
(Born 1880)

JONAS LIE IS TO THE NATIONAL ACADEMY what John Sloan was to the new American school of painting (the necessity for Sloan's battle is now somewhat waning). Lie is as staunch an academician as Sloan is anti-academic. As the peppery president of the National Academy since 1934, his hot-tempered outbursts have been laughed at and gravely considered, but never ignored. The most extreme radical painter has to admit that Lie knows his business, that he is a master technician. His terms as president of the Academy have been notable for Lie's progressive attitude toward younger artists.

In speaking of present-day murals, and particularly of government commissioned murals, he once said: "If the academic tradition is on the skids, then God help American mural painting. Without academic training, we have not much to fall back on. And if a mural painter is to do his work well, he must bend his knees to his master, the architect."

As a painter-member of the Municipal Art Commission in 1935, Lie was called upon to pass on much of the work, and at that time he said: "Some of it I have passed, approved of, because I knew the walls on which it would be painted could very easily be white-washed over. We don't consider the works so entirely permanent, you know. And then, there is always the chance that the old, decrepit buildings which the young are adorning will not outlast our own lifetime."

And then of propaganda in art: "Art is not art when it is propaganda. If in a painting beauty carries more than propaganda, the propaganda is justifiable, but if a painting is merely propaganda in the guise of art, then I say down with it. . . .Treason is no less treason because it is pictorial or literary."

In 1934, worrying about the lack of balance in the art of this country, he said: "It is concentrated here and there, to its own disadvantage, as in New York. We should develop regional interests if we are to nurture a truly native and national art. The individual sectors, with their varied talents and cultures, should be encouraged in their respective movements."

Born in Moss, Norway, Jonas Lie was named after his uncle, the noted novelist and friend of Ibsen. His father was a civil engineer and his mother an American from New England. Lie first wanted to be a musician, and he is today a great lover of music. At the age of twelve he began to study drawing under Christian Skredsvig, a lifelong friend of the family. After his father's death, Jonas Lie was taken to Paris to live with his uncle, and there he attended French school during the day and studied drawing in the evenings. A year later he came to America to live with his mother's family.

At the age of twenty he began exhibiting at the National Academy of Design, after having studied at the Ethical Culture School, the free evening classes at the National Academy, and later at the Art Students' League. In 1912 he was elected associate member of the Academy, thirteen years later was made full academician.

"Color," Lie says, "is the chief medium through which we attain pictorial expression; but color must be interpretative, not imitative. In order to produce lasting work, the actual, visual impression we derive from nature should be less forceful, less vivid, than the accompanying mental impression. I do not attempt voluntarily to symbolize nature, but in portraying nature to impart a sense of what is within and what is beyond."

Lie is represented in many American museums as well as in the Luxembourg Museum.

Old Smuggler's Cove (page 129) shows a village on the Cornish coast of England which Lie visited during the summer of 1937.

WARD LOCKWOOD
(Born 1894)

WARD LOCKWOOD'S PAINTINGS border on the abstract yet retain the humanizing factor of subject matter. He builds realism into an abstract organization of line, color and form, and in the last twelve years has spent an increasing amount of time finishing his pictures without the actual model before him.

This development in his work coincides with Lockwood's settling in Taos, New Mexico, in 1926. He and his wife went there for a three months' visit, bought an old adobe house, remodeled it, and have lived in Taos ever since.

Lockwood studied art at the University of Kansas, Pennsylvania Academy of the Fine Arts, and at the Academy Ransom in Paris. He has taught at the Broadmoor Art Academy (now the Colorado Springs Fine Arts Center), and at the University of California. In 1938 he was appointed Chairman of the Department of Art in the newly established College of Fine Art of the University of Texas.

Lockwood's murals are in the Taos County Court House, Taos; Colorado Springs Fine Arts Center; U. S. Post Office Building in Wichita, Kansas; Post Office Department Building in Washington, D. C. and in the Post Office and Court House Building in Lexington, Kentucky. His easel paintings are in the collections of the Whitney Museum of American Art, the Pennsylvania Academy, Denver Art Museum, and California Palace of the Legion of Honor.

Corner Grocery, Taos (page 76) is Lockwood's own neighborhood grocery. "Every time I have entered this store," he says, "I have had a visual treat in the garish gayety of the brilliantly colored displays of canned goods, labeled bottles and boxes, green vegetables, fruits in yellows, oranges and reds and the gaudy advertising cut-outs." The painting is done in transparent glazes of oil and varnish over a light ground in order to bring out the full power and brilliance of pigment.

LUIGI LUCIONI
(Born 1900)

REALISM, WITH PHOTOGRAPHIC ATTENTION TO DETAIL, characterizes Lucioni's painting. He is a hard worker, painting from sunup to sundown, singing while he works, traits inherited from his Italian peasant parents.

Lucioni was born in Malnate, Italy, a little town north of Milan in the foothills of the Alps. At the age of eleven he came with his family to America to settle in Jersey City. Admitted to Cooper Union when he was sixteen, he studied there for four years, earning his living in the meantime by commercial art work in an engraving house. Sunday mornings he studied painting with William Starkweather. After Cooper Union he was admitted to the National Academy of Design School, where he continued his study for four and a half years. In 1924 he received a Tiffany Foundation Fellowship and at the Foundation's estate on Long Island spent the following nine summers.

Returning to the scenes of his childhood in Italy in 1925 Lucioni saw the Italian primitives and was deeply impressed by their painstaking realism. It was the kind of painting he himself wanted to do. Back in America, he rented a studio in Washington Square and set out to find his own way of painting. He has realized that he must work close to his subject and explains: "I don't say that it is the only way to paint, but for me it is."

Lucioni spends most of his summers in Vermont, whose high rolling hills bring to mind the well-remembered landscape near Malnate, Italy. His devotion to Vermont has made him something of a painter laureate to that state. His paintings are in the following collections: Whitney Museum, Metropolitan Museum, Pennsylvania Academy, William Rockhill Nelson Gallery, Andover Gallery, Canajoharie Museum, Denver Museum and Dartmouth College.

Vermont Classic (page 101) was painted near Shelburne, Vermont.

REGINALD MARSH
(Born 1898)

"THE HAVOC CAUSED BY THE TREMENDOUS INFLUENCE of impressionism and expressionism must be overcome before America can go on and paint the substance, not the light and shadow. The struggle to free art from superficial impressionistic style or fantastic nonsense, is probably harder now than in the old days when art was strong, simple and real." Thus today speaks Reginald Marsh who for years has been struggling to find his own personal way to depict that part of the American Scene that moves him most.

Marsh says: "I like to paint burlesque because it puts together in one picture a nude or near nude woman, baroque architecture for a setting, and a crowd of men, very typical men, for an audience. I like the great Coney Island beach for its infinite number and kinds of people, for the physical manifestations of people from head to toe, its variety of design and its great vitality. Just in this way there is enormous and endless material to paint in New York, exciting, rarely touched, and waiting for the artist to make use of it."

Marsh as an individual personifies America's struggle to free itself artistically. His mother as well as his father, Fred Dana Marsh, were steeped in academic tradition. They were living and painting in Paris in 1898 when Reginald was born, brought him two years later to Nutley, New Jersey. There young Marsh began to draw in his father's studio, where such visitors as Albert Sterner, Ernest Haskell and George Bellows would drop in for an exchange of ideas.

At Yale, where Marsh received his A.B. in 1920, he became a cartoonist on the *Yale Record*. That helped him later to start successfully as a free lance newspaper artist in New York. He was soon drawing for *Vanity Fair* and became staff artist on the *Daily News* for three years, covering vaudeville acts. But the *News* job took little of his time and he was able to develop as an easel painter and scenic designer, and he did special caricature curtains for J. Murray Anderson's Greenwich Village Follies under Robert Edmond Jones. He designed the Provincetown Players "Fashion." In the meantime he was studying drawing at night under John Sloan.

Marsh started to paint in 1923 and of those years he says: "There was a bewildering confusion of style, more than now, facing the novice. I wanted to be a Marin, a Cézanne, a Sloan, a Bouché, or God knows what, but never a *Saturday Evening Post* artist. . . .

"As for the subject, I became, the more I worked, engrossed in the great surrounding panorama of New York. Not being a person of great experience or widely traveled, it was difficult to be aware of contemporary New York's peculiar and tremendous significance, and since our painting showed little of it, I can't exactly say how I came to paint New York, except that determining and articulate encouragement came from my new friend and teacher, Kenneth Hayes Miller, whose scholarly and original mind is the most valuable influence we have. It was he who made me know that art is based on sound tradition.

"Today I am doing my best to discover the principles of the 'great tradition' in order to portray in a sound manner the subjects that move me. I have traveled abroad to many countries to gaze at the Old Masters. It is from them that we must descend. . . ."

Of America's eagerness to find its own way, he says: "There is a quantity of talent but we live our lives half or all the way through before we can see the right track. Education, so important, is hard to find. Schools that suppose themselves founded on the Renaissance seem so counterfeit. Schools that require propaganda becloud the issue. 'Modernistic' schools are for students who like to swoon. . . . What are we going to do?"

But while Marsh has been searching, the results of his findings have not gone unnoticed. In 1936 the Post Office Department in Washington, D. C., commissioned him to paint murals depicting the transfer of mail. And his easel pictures have been acquired by the Metropolitan Museum, Whitney Museum, Addison Gallery, University of Nebraska, Springfield Museum, the Pennsylvania Academy, Lenox Art Association, Art Institute of Chicago, Hartford Atheneum, and the Boston Museum.

High Yaller (page 81) is typical of the lusty technique with which Marsh highlights the picturesque aspects of New York life. Marsh is an energetic worker. After the sketches for the post office murals reproduced in this book were approved, it took him just twenty-one days to paint the 13½ by 7 ft. panels directly on wet plaster. Postal officials could find no flaw in *Sorting Mail* (page 80). They did quibble, however, over details in *Transfer of Mail from Liner to Tugboat* (page 80), pointing out that when incoming foreign mail is being transferred from liner to mail boat, the red-striped registered sacks are never heaped with ordinary sacks. The government paid Marsh $3,000, of which almost half went for materials.

HENRY E. MATTSON
(Born 1887)

EXPLAINING HIS DRAMATIC PAINTINGS of the sea, Henry Mattson says: "The feeling I had was created by the threatening quality in deep dark water. You don't see this threat, you feel it. That's the feeling I painted." He is, he says, a metaphysical painter, "interested in the reality not in the appearance of things. I paint without any visual suggestion from given objects. My painting grows from a blank canvas to its completion from my inner consciousness. I feel that painting should be liberated from literal reporting—thus only can an artist truly express himself freely in his work."

Born in Sweden, Mattson came to this country when he was nineteen and studied art at the Worcester Museum while working as a mechanic. In 1916 he joined the Woodstock art colony, and has lived there ever since.

Mattson has painted two murals for the Portland, Maine, post office, won a Guggenheim Fellowship in 1935. He is represented in the Metropolitan Museum, Whitney Museum, St. Louis Art Museum, Detroit Institute of Art, Newark Museum, Phillips Memorial Gallery, and has a picture in the White House. He painted his emotional canvas, *Night and the Sea* (page 127) in Woodstock where, far from the ocean, he paints from imagination most of his seascapes.

JOHN McCRADY
(Born 1911)

"WITHOUT THE SLIGHTEST IDEA of what I wanted to paint," says McCrady, "I went north in 1933 to the Art Students' League. I painted people but they were just people and there was no reason for them. I drew pictures of New York: subways, burlesque shows, dirty waterfronts, vulgar people—everything other students were doing.

But I found no pleasure in it; I began to feel I'd made a mistake to think I'd ever be an artist." He yearned for his home in the South as the bitter New York winter days grew long. McCrady continues: "I could see Oxford (Mississippi) on top of the hill, its towering steeples, the courthouse in the center, the tolling of the courthouse clock that could be heard for miles about by the laughing and singing negroes sweating in the cotton fields beneath the boiling sun." Then, for the first time, he began to paint that which he knew.

He returned home, set up a studio in old New Orleans and there today he paints his nostalgic scenes of the Deep South.

McCrady was born in the Episcopal rectory of Canton, Mississippi, the seventh child of a Southern clergyman. All his childhood was spent in Southern towns. He studied at the University of Mississippi, got his first professional art training at the University of Pennsylvania, and later on with a fellowship entered the Art Students' League. He had not seen an original work of art until he was nineteen.

McCrady believes that "man has no world to paint but his own. I can't see the sense of going from place to place in search of something new and interesting. In one small Mississippi town I find unlimited material to paint. I probably will remain in the South, feeling as I do that some day out of this section will come a very wholesome and good art."

His works are in the collections of the City Art Museum of St. Louis, Missouri; High Museum of Art, Atlanta, Georgia; and the Southeastern Louisiana College. His *Swing Low, Sweet Chariot* (page 99) shows an old negro dying as black angels come to take his soul up to heaven. Note the struggling red devil on the sidelines.

GEORGIA O'KEEFFE
(Born 1887)

SOME CRITICS HAVE CALLED GEORGIA O'KEEFFE the most renowned of living American women painters; others have described her work as purely decorative. Into neat, orderly abstractions she has studiously simplified such real objects as roses in full bloom, morning glories, feathers, skulls and strange black crosses—most of them on a gigantic scale. Though she claims never to have read Freud, many of her admirers read Freudian symbols into her work. She has never been to Europe and says she has never had the desire to go. America, she says, can give her all she wants.

O'Keeffe was born in Sun Prairie, Wisconsin, the daughter of an Irish farmer and Hungarian mother. With her parents, four sisters and two brothers she moved in 1901 to Williamsburg, Virginia. Three years later she was studying art at the Chicago Art Institute, and the following year entered the Art Students' League in New York. In 1906, discouraged, she abandoned fine art as a career, did not paint seriously again for almost ten years. In the meantime she worked at various advertising agencies, studied at Teachers College in New York and taught drawing in Virginia. Later she went to Amarillo, Texas, to teach, and there drew the fateful sketches she sent to her friend, Anita Pollitzer, in New York. This friend took them to the then famous gallery at 291 Fifth Avenue where Alfred Stieglitz reigned as the high priest of modern French art.

Stieglitz insisted on exhibiting the drawings. From then on Georgia O'Keeffe's career was linked with that of the noted impresario-photographer. For a time O'Keeffe sent her drawings to Stieglitz from Texas, but finally decided to move to New York. She wanted to paint but had no money. Stieglitz loaned her $1,200 and in 1920 she held her first important show. It was a success. She married Stieglitz four years later.

Stieglitz has sold most of O'Keeffe's pictures only to intimate admirers. Among public institutions, the Whitney, Cleveland, Detroit and Brooklyn Museums and the Phillips Memorial Gallery in Washington own her work. As in the *White Barn* (page 124), simplicity of line and purity of tone characterize O'Keeffe's paintings, the essentials being abstracted from the mass of detail. There are many such immaculate white barns between Montreal and Quebec.

WILLIAM C. PALMER
(Born 1906)

DURING THE BOOM YEARS Palmer made a good living as an interior decorator. Then came the depression and he was forced back to painting merely for the sake of painting. Today he is one of the best known younger mural and easel painters, and is an instructor at the Art Students' League.

Like so many of his contemporaries, Palmer first gained recognition when he began to paint scenes that really stirred him personally. The depression forced him to retire for a while to the home of his sister in Canada where he began to paint nostalgic scenes of his childhood—Iowa landscapes. During the summer of 1932 he returned to Iowa to gather material for a series of canvases. These were exhibited that year in his first one-man show, so successfully that the exhibition was invited to Washington, D. C., and made a tour of the Middle West. The following year the Whitney Museum bought one of his canvases.

In 1933, working for the Public Works Art Project, he designed a mural, *Function of a Hospital*, probably the first mural ever painted around such a theme. This was later installed in the Queens General Hospital, and in 1936 Palmer painted fourteen panels for the same hospital depicting the *Development of Medicine*.

At this time he was put on the WPA as a non-relief supervisor in charge of a mural project at $23 a week. The following year he was invited by the Section of Fine Art of the Treasury Department to paint mural decorations for the new Post Office Building in Washington, D. C., and in 1938 he completed a mural for the post office lobby in Arlington, Mass. In the meantime he continued his easel painting, held another one-man show in 1938 in New York, one in Des Moines, Iowa, in 1939, and conducted classes at the Art Students' League since 1937.

The Palmer family first came to America in 1629, when Walter Palmer helped settle Stonington, Connecticut. William Palmer's ancestors were for the most part physicians and clergymen who followed the frontier to the west. His paternal great-grandfather and grandfather were physicians in Illinois and Iowa. His father, also a doctor, finally settled in Des Moines, Iowa, and there William Palmer was born in 1906.

Controlled Medicine (page 104) shows the application of preventive medicine. At left are internes with ether and oxygen tank. Back of them is a sterilizer. At center an operating light and a counterlight with ultraviolet rays to sterilize the air shine on a child being vaccinated. At right is a doctor with a stethoscope. At far right are an X-ray machine and several doctors wearing leather aprons over smocks to keep the dangerous rays from penetrating. The scene is a far cry from Rembrandt's *Anatomy Lesson* and Eakins' *Gross Clinic*.

WALDO PEIRCE
(Born 1884)

WALDO PEIRCE IS AS WELL KNOWN FOR HIS ESCAPADES as for his happy, Renoiresque paintings. Perhaps his best known adventure resulted from his impulsive decision to sail to Europe on a cattle boat in 1911 with his Harvard friend, the revolutionist John Reed. The trip ended when Peirce changed his mind, jumped overboard and swam back to Boston. The stunt caused the temporary arrest of Reed for the supposed murder of his missing friend.

Peirce was born in Bangor, Maine, the son of a wealthy lumber man. He graduated from Harvard in 1906 (where he starred on the football team), and then studied painting in Paris at the old Julian Academy. In 1912 he journeyed to Spain and settled in an old church which the Spanish painter, Zuloaga, had transformed into a studio. During the World War he drove an ambulance in France. He was wounded, refused a commission, and was decorated with the Croix de Guerre. After the war he returned to Spain with his friend, Ernest Hemingway.

At the end of thirty lusty years of painting, traveling, and adventuring, during which time he turned out hundreds of swiftly painted, highly emotional canvases, Peirce returned to America where he now divides his time between Bangor and Haverstraw, New York. With him are his third wife, the painter Alzira Peirce (twenty-four years his junior), and their three much-painted youngsters: Michael and Chamberlain, who are twins, and Anna Gabrielle.

With his return to America and his plunge into domesticity after three decades of adventuring, Peirce has gained a new depth and tenderness in his art. Today his pictures are an interpretation of the rustic family life of sophisticated people who have returned to the soil. The artist's new phase has gained wide recognition and he is represented in the Metropolitan Museum, the Whitney Museum, the Addison Gallery of American Art and the Pennsylvania Academy.

Maine Trotting Race (page 78) is a glimpse of action at a Maine rural fair. It is typical of Peirce's new interest in his native country.

HENRY VARNUM POOR
(Born 1888)

EARTHY MATERIALISM PLUS CREATIVE FIRE have made Henry Varnum Poor one of America's most versatile artists. Potter and craftsman as well as painter, he has also built houses, fountains, lamp bases, designed tiles for interior decoration and architectural purposes, and carved furniture. He designed and built the rambling timber and stone house in the High Tor country near Nyack, N. Y. where he lives with his son and novelist wife, Bessie Breuer.

Intellectual rather than emotional, his paintings are direct statements of fact. Of New England ancestry, Henry Varnum Poor was born in Chapman, Kansas, the son of a banker and grain broker. He traveled through Europe on a bicycle, went to London to study French as well as art before he

Rehearsal—Frederic Taubes

The Pink Skirt—GLADYS ROCKMORE DAVIS

The Blue Necklace—EUGENE SPEICHER

Nude—ANN BROCKMAN

The Dancer—JERRY FARNSWORTH

Arrangement, Life and Still Life—ROBERT BRACKMAN

Objects on Sofa—Yasuo Kuniyoshi

My Wife—Richard Lahey

Mural Assistant—Louis Bouché

Basket and Fruit—ARNOLD BLANCH

Figure Outdoors—LEON KROLL

Katharine Hepburn—ALEXANDER BROOK

Katharine Cornell as Candida—EUGENE SPEICHER

White Lace—JOHN CARROLL

attempted Julian's Academy in Paris. In the spring of 1911 he won a portrait contest at Julian's. On his return to America, Poor taught art at Stanford University. Later he became an instructor at the Mark Hopkins Institute, now known as the California School of Fine Arts.

During the World War Poor was drafted into the Army. After the War he held his first show, sold only one picture, and decided that a living could not be made from painting. He turned to the less-crowded field of pottery, bought the six acres of land in Nyack where he now lives, made himself a potter's wheel, installed a kiln and from his land dug the native red clay he uses in his ceramics. His first crude bowls sold immediately. He perfected glazes and worked out his own decorative schemes. He prospered, went to southern France for a year and turned again to painting.

In 1935 the Treasury Department's Section of Fine Art commissioned him to do the murals in the corridors of the Post Office and Justice Department buildings in Washington, D. C., for which he received about $20 a square foot. The panels reproduced in this book (page 82) are 13 feet high by 3 feet wide. On the *Tennessee Valley Authority* panel the man coming home from work to his family is George Biddle. The *Gold Case* panel aroused debate in Washington because the lawyer has turned his back on Chief Justice Hughes and Justices Brandeis and McReynolds. In the middle distance, head on hand, Poor has portrayed himself.

EDNA REINDEL
(Born 1900)

EDNA REINDEL'S INTELLECTUAL AND CAREFULLY RESTRAINED PICTURES have steadily gained recognition. Known mostly for her flowers and still-life studies, she has recently painted a series of New England scenes at Martha's Vineyard, where she has spent the last few summers.

Miss Reindel was born in Detroit and studied at Pratt Institute, N. Y. Upon graduation in 1923 she did book illustration and free-lance commercial art work for five years. Since her studies on a Tiffany Foundation Fellowship and her first one-man show in New York in 1934 she has painted a mural for the Stamford, Conn., Housing Project, and is now working on a Treasury Department mural for the post office of Swainsboro, Georgia. She teaches painting to private pupils.

Her paintings are owned by the Whitney Museum, the Metropolitan Museum and Ball State Teacher's College, among other public institutions. *New England Harbor* (page 79) depicts Menemsha Bight, near the western end of Martha's Vineyard. Menemsha is a port for many Vineyard fishermen, but it attracts more artists than tourists. Note the floating markers stacked up in front of the lobster-man's shed. Lobstermen use these to locate and identify lobster pots. *New England Harbor*, typical of the artist's crisp, clean cut forms, is owned by David Levins of New York City.

ALBERT PINKHAM RYDER
(Born 1847, Died 1917)

RYDER SHARES WITH HOMER AND EAKINS the distinction of being an American old master. In an incredibly dirty New York studio he painted his dreams and turned out some of the finest work in the history of American painting.

Though able to devote his entire time to painting (he had a small but adequate income), Ryder completed less than two hundred canvases during his seventy years. Once while working on a canvas that had been in progress for a long time, he was told that he could become prosperous if he would produce more prolifically. In reply Ryder locked himself in his studio and painted a few more years on the same canvas. After working eighteen years on *Macbeth and the Witches*, he said, "I think the sky is getting interesting."

Ryder felt no need to travel for inspiration. In 1893, Cottier, the Scotch art dealer, took him abroad, but Ryder studied the sea rather than the museums. He returned claiming that the Palisades and Central Park gave him all that he wanted. For many years he lived and painted in a small room in the Hotel Albert on University Place in New York. The hotel was owned by a brother who named it after the painter.

Ryder was a descendant of seven generations of mechanics, sailors and shopkeepers, and was born in New Bedford, Mass. Poor business drove his father to New York after Albert (he was called Pinkie) Ryder finished grammar school. In the meantime impure vaccine had injured his eyes, and he suffered from poor eyesight for the rest of his life.

The elder Ryder tried his hand at many trades, and after failing at everything "was persuaded to forego the luxury of supporting himself." Thereafter, Albert Ryder's brother supported the entire family and became proprietor of the Hotel Albert. It was to this brother that the painter owed his support.

In New York Ryder studied painting for a while with William E. Marshall. He attended the National Academy in 1871 but soon walked out on the school, refusing to draw from antique casts. Thirty-five years later, however, he became an N.A. and exhibited at the Academy.

As an individual Ryder was as eccentric as were his canvases poetic and mysterious. It is said that he believed that association with people made him unfit for painting, and therefore preferred to spend his time by himself, alone with his paintings. In describing one of his early landscapes, he said: "I saw nature springing into life upon my dead canvas. It was better than nature, for it was vibrant with the thrill of a new creation."

Ryder fell ill in 1915, and after a prolonged stay at St. Vincent's Hospital, was moved to the home of a friend at Elmhurst, Long Island. It was Ryder's first trip away from New York City since his trip to Europe. At his friend's home he died.

Death on a Pale Horse (page 22), now owned by the Cleveland Museum, was inspired by the suicide of the artist's favorite waiter at the Hotel Albert, because of racetrack debts.

ROBERT W. SALMON
(Born about 1800)

VERY LITTLE IS KNOWN of the life of this English-born marine painter who came to America in 1829. He was active in Boston as late as 1840, painting such scenes as *The Wharves of Boston*, which now hangs in the old Boston State House, and *Rocks at Nahant*. owned by the Boston Museum of Fine Arts.

Boston Harbor—Long and Central Wharves (page 18), painted in 1832, belongs to Henry R. Dalton. It shows Boston when it was the shipping center of the new United States empire of commerce and when its jungle of masts teemed with emigrants, merchants and sailors unloading cargoes.

PAUL SAMPLE
(Born 1896)

AS ARTIST-IN-RESIDENCE at Dartmouth College Sample says of his early life:
"I was born in Louisville, Kentucky, and lived all over the United States as my father was a construction engineer. I graduated from Dartmouth College in 1921 after wasting my time intensively for a number of years as is customary for the average college student. I was much more interested in holding the college heavyweight boxing championship and playing on the football team than anything else. I took an art appreciation course and slept through it every day. I never drew nor painted.

"During the World War I served a couple of years in the Navy, went back to school afterwards. But the year I got out I had a relapse with a bad lung and spent the next four years hospitalized in Saranac Lake. It gave me a good chance to do some thinking and led to the decision to do what I had always wanted to do—paint."

In 1925 Sample left Saranac and studied in New York for a few months, then went to California. "I studied out there," he says. "But I couldn't stomach the practice of painting a lot of High Sierras and desert flowers which seemed to be the only kind of pictures that were sold there. I had no money, but the worst was the constant thought that at my age I should be working at something profitable and gaining some economic security. My mother and father were sympathetic but I suffered agonies of doubt. I didn't have the remotest idea how my work would develop or whether I had anything." Then Sample got a part-time job teaching drawing and painting at the art school of the University of Southern California, and began to exhibit. His reputation soon became nation-wide.

Last year, on his first vacation in sixteen years, Sample went to Europe with his Vermont-born wife, the former Sylvia Ann Howland, and studied the Flemish and Italian masters. Returning as Artist-in-Residence at Dartmouth, he finds himself still experimenting, and says: "Although my work now is not imitative of nature or representational in character, it is not abstract and I have always felt a strong urge to combine the literal or story-telling aspect in some degree with the purely aesthetic elements in a picture."

Sample's pictures may be seen in the Metropolitan Museum, the Springfield (Mass.) Museum, the Canajoharie Gallery, the West Museum at Swarthmore College, the Wood Art Gallery in Montpelier, Vt., the University of Southern California, the University of Minnesota and the White House. *Janitor's Holiday* (page 75) was painted in Montpelier. The man reclining under the tree in the bright fall sunlight is Henry Davidson, janitor of the building where Sample had his studio. The Metropolitan Museum bought this picture in 1937, and Mrs. Davidson made a special trip to New York "to see Henry in the Metropolitan."

JOHN SINGER SARGENT
(Born 1856, Died 1925)

SARGENT, MOST FAMOUS FASHIONABLE PORTRAIT PAINTER OF HIS AGE, did not set foot on American soil until he was twenty.
Sargent was born in Florence, Italy, of American parents. His mother, a painter of water colors, encouraged him to copy the Old Masters in European museums. When he was eighteen he went to Paris to study, and two years later made his first trip to the United States.

After a period in Spain and North Africa, Sargent settled in Paris where he began his career as portrait painter. There he remained until he painted the portrait of Madame Gautreau, better known as *Madame X.* This portrait in 1884 was considered so realistic and true to life that Sargent was showered with unwelcome criticism. His pride stung, the painter left for England and made that country his home for the rest of his life.

In 1890, when he was thirty-four, Sargent was commissioned by the Public Library of Boston to paint a set of murals. To gather material for these, he first visited Egypt and then returned to paint the murals in his studio just outside London. He completed them twenty-six years later. Just before his death Sargent painted another set of mural decorations for the Boston Museum.

During the World War he made a series of quick impressionistic scenes behind the lines. With his spinster sister (he never married) Sargent was making plans for a visit to the United States when he died quietly in his sleep.

The Wyndham Sisters (page 41) were the daughters of the late Honorable Percy Scawen Wyndham, who was the third son of Lord Leconfield. One daughter, the Countess of Wemyss and March, died April 1937, aged seventy-four. Another sister, Pamela, was the second wife of the late Viscount Grey of Fallodon. She died in 1928. The third sister, Madeline, is Mrs. George Adeane. This portrait was Sargent's contribution to the Royal Academy in 1900. The popular name, *The Three Graces,* was given the picture by King Edward VII in a spontaneous tribute to the sisters' beauty. The Metropolitan Museum bought the picture in March, 1927, from Captain G.R.C. Wyndham of London, nephew of the sisters, for $90,000.

CHARLES SHEELER
(Born 1883)

JUST AS HE HAS TRIED to combine abstraction and realism, so has Sheeler worked to combine photography and painting. With the camera he earned his living until 1931, photographing houses for architects' records. This was in line with his interest in structural form, and his passion for finding beauty in commonplace things and depicting strictly functional objects with exactitude.

Sheeler was born in Philadelphia of an old Pennsylvania family, and there for three years attended the Philadelphia School of Industrial Art. For the next three years he studied at the Philadelphia Academy, spending his summers in Europe studying the Old Masters. He returned to support himself with photography, painting over week-ends in Bucks County, Pennsylvania. There the early American architecture and furniture inspired him to paint chairs, tables, stairways, machinery and kitchen utensils with an almost religious preoccupation with form and detail. In 1927 he spent six weeks photographing the Ford plant at River Rouge, and ten years later made paintings of the scene. Sheeler was among the first to paint the American industrial scene.

Sheeler's pictures are owned by the Museum of Modern Art, Art Institute of Chicago, Whitney Museum, Fogg Museum, Boston Museum, Springfield Museum of Fine Arts, Worcester Museum, among others. Sheeler painted *City Interior* (page 126), a study of the Ford plant at River Rouge, after ten years of reflection on United States industrialism. Note the patterns formed by overhead conveyors, tracks, pipes, roofs and the play of light. It is one of Sheeler's most intricate works.

JOHN SLOAN
(Born 1871)

SO THOROUGHLY ACCEPTED IS JOHN SLOAN as an heroic figure in contemporary American art that he is neglected. As the father of this generation of American painters he is loved and respected, but like the head of a great and robust family, he is taken for granted. And, therefore, though it was he more than any other artist who fought for and helped win the battles of contemporary American art back in pre-war days, he cannot be classed among the more financially successful painters.

John Sloan was one of the first to paint his own environment. And so absorbed has he been in the American Scene that he has never crossed either ocean. As a teacher and painter he has literally raised generations of painters who, famous now in their own right, swear by him as a source of inspiration.

And to many John Sloan represents not only art, but glamor and the good old days in Greenwich Village when life was hearty and good, and there were Petitpas, Romany Marie, and McSorley's Bar. And, of course, Washington Square and the bull sessions where lusty verbal fights were waged for the old *Masses*, for liberty of speech, and, above all, liberty of art. Sloan, always a fighter, battled mightily against academic painting. He has been the fighting president of the Society of Independent Artists since 1918. He helped start the group out of which grew the famous Armory Show in 1913, bringing "modernism" to America.

Sloan was born in Lock Haven, Pennsylvania. When he was six, his father moved the family to Philadelphia, where Sloan senior went into the stationery business. In Philadelphia, at Central High School, Albert C. Barnes (famed now for his Argerol millions, for the Barnes Foundation, and for his wonderfully unprintable letters), William Glackens, and Sloan were fellow students. Now both Glackens and Sloan have paintings in the Barnes collection, and it was to Barnes that Sloan, at forty-three, sold his first painting, *Nude, Green Scarf*.

At sixteen Sloan went to work for a bookseller, attended art classes at night at the Spring Garden Institute. Later he studied at night at the Pennsylvania Academy of the Fine Arts. His father hoped he would become a dentist. At twenty he tried unsuccessfully to earn his living as a free-lance illustrator, and that year he made his first etching. He got a $20-a-week job on the Philadelphia *Inquirer* and stayed there three years. During the following four years he worked on the Philadelphia *Press*, left that for the New York *Herald*, only to return to the Philadelphia *Press*, where he worked until 1904.

In 1905 Sloan arrived in New York to stay. He sketched for the *Century Magazine*, for *McClure's*, *Colliers*, and *Everybody's*, drew posters, and did illustrations for books. In the meantime he was painting, but did not turn to serious painting until he was thirty, after his canvas *Independence Square, Philadelphia* was exhibited at the Carnegie International. He was made instructor at the Art Students' League in 1914, remained there to teach until 1930. In 1915 he was made president of the League. Sloan has never drawn, etched, or painted a still-life. He painted his first landscape in Gloucester, where he vacationed during 1914 and 1915. Since 1919 he and his wife, Dolly Sloan, have spent the summers in Santa Fe where they have a beautiful pink adobe house. He has just completed a government mural for the Bronxville, N. Y., post office.

Sloan is represented in the Metropolitan Museum, Whitney Museum, Detroit Institute, Brooklyn Museum, Art Institute of Chicago, and many other public collections.

Sunday, Women Drying Their Hair (page 43) and *Wake of the Ferry No. 2* (page 44), sturdy in their realism, exemplify Sloan at his best when he was a driving force of "The Eight" of 1908.

RAPHAEL SOYER
(Born 1899)

RICH TEXTURES AND SOFT FORMS save Raphael Soyer's moody, down-trodden New York subjects from being solely Social Protest pictures. A few years ago, one of the most ardent of left-wing painters, he now believes: "It is ridiculous to paint what is not before you, but it is equally futile to paint social content pictures consciously." The subjects for Soyer's poignant pictures are usually the less fortunate habitués of New York City's Fourteenth Street where he has his studio on the fifth floor of an old ramshackle building.

Raphael Soyer came to America from Tombov, Russia, with his father, mother, three brothers and two sisters, just before the World War. His father, a Hebrew teacher and writer, gave him most of his schooling. He had to leave high school to earn his living as errand boy, newsboy, and factory worker in an embroidery shop. Soyer studied nights at Cooper Union, and later trained at the National Academy and at the Art Students' League. His brothers, Isaac and Moses, are also well-known painters.

Raphael Soyer's pictures are in the collections of the Metropolitan Museum, Whitney Museum, New York Public Library, Columbus Museum, Newark Museum, Addison Gallery, Duncan Phillips Memorial Gallery and the National Gallery at Oslo, Norway. *Doctor's Office* (page 105), a richly textured canvas in which subject, mood and color are in perfect harmony, may be termed a plea for socialized medicine.

EUGENE SPEICHER
(Born 1883)

SPEICHER LOOKS LIKE A LUMBERMAN and he almost became one. After attending public and high schools in Buffalo, N. Y., where he was born, Speicher got a job in a lumber yard. He did so well that he was soon earning $28 a week, and he was on his way toward a successful lumberman's career. In the meantime he was studying nights at the Albright Art School. To be at the lumber yard by 6:45 in the morning he had to get up at 5 A.M. He left work at 5:30 P.M., rushed to the local Y.M.C.A. for a game of basketball before dinner, and immediately after dinner hurried off to art classes which lasted until 11 P.M. He did this for a year. Then he sold a picture for $35 to the director of the Buffalo Art Gallery, won a scholarship to the Art Students' League in New York, and decided to become a painter. He spent his first day in New York at the 57th Street Y.M.C.A. gym.

Speicher indicated his flair for portraiture from the very beginning when he won a prize at the League for a portrait of a fellow student, Patsy O'Keeffe, now better known as Georgia O'Keeffe. Speicher also won a scholarship allowing him a second year of free tuition at the League. He spent that year (1908) studying under William Chase and Frank Dumond. Though he was still a student, galleries were already exhibiting his canvases. To earn his way, he pitched hay during summers, and made quick portraits at three sittings for $25, taking on all comers. The following year (1909) he met Robert Henri, who was conducting classes in the then famous Lincoln Arcade Building and influencing modern American painting through such students as George Bellows and Guy Pène du Bois. A year later Speicher married and settled in Woodstock, so poor that he had to make his furniture from the packing cases in which he had shipped his pictures.

Today he recalls the years between 1910 and 1915 as the hardest. Though he had already won prizes, and was becoming well known as a portraitist, he got only a few commissions. By 1920, however, he was well on his way to becoming one of America's most successful portrait painters. Nine years later he was doing so well that he was refusing commissions except those that particularly inspired him. He could probably become as popular and wealthy as Sargent had been, but he would rather paint only what pleases him. He says: "I don't want a lot of money. I don't need it. I live a simple life."

The Speichers spend seven months a year in Woodstock, five winter months in New York. In the summer Speicher paints four or five hours a day, regularly takes afternoons off for golf. In the winter he keeps fit by squash and tennis. Every five years he holds a one-man show, and then the Speichers go abroad. Speicher has been to every country in Europe except Soviet Russia and Sweden. His paintings are owned by twenty-seven American museums, among them the Metropolitan, Albright Gallery, Cleveland Museum, Corcoran Gallery, Detroit Institute of Arts, Fogg Museum at Harvard and the Whitney Museum.

Katharine Cornell as Candida (page 153) is one of Speicher's best known portraits. It belongs to the Museum of Modern Art. *The Blue Necklace* (page 148) owned by the Toledo Museum, which loaned it to the Carnegie Institute for their International show in 1937. Speicher has contributed to the International since 1912.

FREDERIC TAUBES
(Born 1900)

SO POPULAR HAVE TAUBES' POETIC CANVASES BECOME that within six months after his last one-man show in 1938, five American museums and museum directors bought his paintings.

Frederic Taubes was born in Austria, the son of a Viennese banker. He was drawing before he could read or write, and at the age of six was given art lessons. By the time he was ten he already had a good knowledge of anatomy. He was less brilliant, however, in school, and after failing to pass his high school exams when he was eighteen, he ran away to live in a studio shack in the Austrian Tyrol. There he painted landscapes and lived by poaching game from the forest.

Finally Taubes' father agreed to let him continue his painting, gave him a small allowance and sent him to study at the Academy of Munich. There followed training and painting in Weimar, Berlin, Paris, and Italy, and for four years Taubes painted cubistic and dada pictures. Then came post-war inflation chaos, and Taubes' family was ruined. The painter became in rapid succession a sign painter, a poster artist, a magazine illustrator. He sold cotton, license patents, and became a professional guide for ski parties in Switzerland. In the meantime he continued his easel painting. In 1925 he worked as artist-reporter on a Viennese newspaper until he fled what he terms "the cataclysm and ruins of the Danube," traveled as an itinerant painter in Europe and finally landed in New York and became an American citizen.

Because of his technical knowledge he is much sought after as a teacher. His private art classes in his New York studio are crowded with students, and he was appointed art instructor at Mills College, California for the summer of 1939. He believes that painters must "go back to the Old Masters to revive a wisdom and knowledge long since forgotten."

Taubes' paintings are owned by the Bloomington (Illinois) Art Association, the San Diego Fine Arts Gallery and the San Francisco Museum of Art. His favorite model is his blonde Viennese wife who is shown with a valuable Eighteenth Century Stainer violin in *Rehearsal* (page 147). Taubes often works fourteen hours at a stretch. His wife fainted after posing three hours for *Rehearsal*. The model for the flute player actually posed holding a paint brush.

JOHN TRUMBULL
(Born 1756, Died 1843)

MANY AMERICANS VISUALIZE the great events of the Revolution through the eyes of John Trumbull, who, during the War, was Washington's second aide-de-camp. A moody son of a Connecticut governor, he once refused a commission in Washington's army because a clerk misdated it. He graduated from Harvard College in 1773, taught for a short time, then began drilling his friends in the Connecticut troops, and was later appointed aide-de-camp on General Washington's staff.

Leaving the Army to take up painting, Trumbull spent the winter of 1778 in Boston, where friends urged him to go to London to study with Benjamin West. He took this advice in 1780, and armed with a letter of introduction to West from Benjamin Franklin, he sailed for England. There as an American officer he was arrested and put in prison. West, after a personal plea to King George III, brought about his release and he was deported.

After the War, however, in 1784, Trumbull returned to study with West. It was in West's London studio that he painted his *Battle of Bunker Hill,* the *Death of General Montgomery* and the *Declaration of Independence.* For the latter he used sketches made from life. He then went to Paris to paint at firsthand the portraits of French officers for his *Surrender of Lord Cornwallis* (page 17). In 1794 Trumbull entered politics as secretary to John Jay who was then Ambassador to Great Britain. In 1804 he settled in New York, where he painted the portraits of John Jay and Alexander Hamilton, the latter from a portrait bust. Back in England again in 1808, he was forced to remain for the duration of the War of 1812. Returning to New York he was commissioned to paint four pictures for the Capitol at Washington, D. C., for $32,000. He worked on these for eight years, named them: *Declaration of Independence,* the *Surrender of General Burgoyne,* the *Surrender of Lord Cornwallis,* and *Washington Resigning His Commission.* They were installed in 1824.

Trumbull's prosperous days were now over. Aged seventy-six, he found few purchasers and had no important commission. Friends, headed by the elder Professor Benjamin Silliman, induced him to make replicas of his Capitol pictures, and these, with other paintings, were turned over to Yale College in return for which Trumbull received an annuity of $1,000. A friendly skipper transported the collection gratis by sea from New York to New Haven. With this collection Yale founded its art gallery, and there in a vault beneath the fine arts building the old painter was buried.

The *Surrender of Lord Cornwallis* shows General Lincoln (center) leading dismounted British officers through the French (left) and American (right) staffs.

FREDERICK JUDD WAUGH
(Born 1861)

AMERICA'S MOST POPULAR ACADEMIC PAINTER of seascapes is seventy-eight-year-old Frederick Judd Waugh. Winner of the Carnegie International popularity prize for five years in succession, he says: "Not one of my pictures has ever completely satisfied me. I hope that some day I can paint one picture of which I can say, 'This is the sea.'"

Son of portrait painter S. B. Waugh and miniature painter Mary Eliza Young Waugh, he is of Scotch-Irish descent, born in Bordentown, New Jersey. As a child he ran away from school until allowed to study painting, first at the Pennsylvania Academy of Fine Arts, later at the old Julian Academy in Paris. In the early 1900s, in Great Britain, he began painting the type of seascapes he has made so popular.

Tall, slender, with a Van Dyke beard and hazel eyes, he lives all the year round at Provincetown where he has two studios by the sea. He dislikes crowds, rarely appears at the openings of his own art exhibitions. In one of his studios he does his "hobby" painting, which consists of anything that comes to his mind from abstractions to very cluttered canvases of weird objects of art. In the other studio he does his sea paintings. Oddly, his sea painting studio does not look out upon the ocean, but his "hobby" studio commands a magnificent view of the sea. He has a talented artist son, Coulton, who is a "modernist," and a daughter who is a stylist.

Waugh is represented in many American museums as well as in England's Bristol Academy, and the Walker Art Gallery in Liverpool.

The Big Water (page 125), characteristic of Waugh's marine technique, was third in his unbroken string of popular awards at the Carnegie Institute, where the American public can vote on what it likes in art. In 1934, 1935, 1936, 1937 and 1938 they liked Waugh best.

BENJAMIN WEST
(Born 1738, Died 1820)

WHEN WEST AT THE AGE OF SIXTEEN shocked his parents by announcing his intention of becoming an artist, a special meeting of the Society of Friends was held in Springfield Township, Pennsylvania. Painting pictures was not in accord with the tenets of that religious sect, to which his family belonged. But West won out and opened a studio in Philadelphia. Friendly neighborhood Indians had shown West how to use paint, and he is said to have made his first brushes from the hairs of a cat.

With the help of friends, he sailed for Italy when he was twenty-two, and for three years copied Old Masters, particularly Titian. Then he left for London, settled there, and never returned to America. But before leaving America West had won the heart of a Miss Elizabeth Shewell, who insisted on joining him in spite of her family's protests. She finally sailed for London, where they were married.

Through the Archbishop of York, West met King George III, who was so impressed that he made West his historical painter. After the death of Sir Joshua Reynolds, West was made the second president of the Royal Academy—just thirty-four years before his pupil, Samuel F. B. Morse became first president of the National Academy in New York.

First American painter to win fame abroad, West was teacher to two generations of young Americans who went to London to study.

After West's wife died in 1817, his health began to fail and he gave up painting. He died in 1820 and was buried with great ceremony in St. Paul's Cathedral. West painted some 3,000 pictures.

The Death of Wolfe (page 17), now owned by the National Gallery in Ottawa, was criticized because West dressed his characters in contemporary costumes instead of Greek robes or Roman togas. The painting was first bought by Lord Grosvenor while George III was trying to make up his mind as to whether or not he ought to buy it. When the picture was hailed a popular success, the King commanded West to paint a replica. West painted six. The picture on page 19 is the original version. It was presented to Canada in 1918 as a war memorial by the Duke of Westminster, great-great-grandson of Lord Grosvenor. West shows the mortally wounded Wolfe dying after the battle that resulted in the capture of Quebec from the French by the British.

JAMES ABBOTT McNEILL WHISTLER
(Born 1834, Died 1903)

WHISTLER SPENT ONLY SIXTEEN OF HIS SIXTY-NINE YEARS in the United States. In his day he was called a poseur, a crack-pot, a dandy, an eccentric snob, and Europe's greatest painter. He reveled in the limelight and to encourage talk about himself would leave his home in London carrying two umbrellas, a light and a dark one, for rain or sunshine. He used to keep a pocket filled with monocles which he would affix one after another to his eye while talking.

He was born in Lowell, Mass. of Irish-American parents. When he was nine his engineer father, a Major in the U. S. Army, took him to St. Petersburg (Leningrad) Russia, where the elder Whistler had gone to build a railway for Emperor Nicholas. There for a while at the Academy of Fine Arts young Whistler took drawing lessons. Then his mother sent him to study art in London.

After his father's death in 1849, Whistler returned with his mother to the United States to live in Pomfret, Connecticut. When he was seventeen his family insisted that he follow the Whistler family tradition and become a soldier. Whistler was sent to West Point where for three years, under General Robert E. Lee, he reveled in military atmosphere but refused to submit to military discipline. Finally, failing in chemistry, he was dismissed. For a while he worked as a draftsman in the Coast Survey Department at Washington for $1.50 a day. But he disliked the tedious job and persuaded his mother to send him to France to study art. She gave him an allowance of $350 a year and Whistler left America, never again to return.

In Paris he studied two years with Charles Gabriel Gleyre, then decided he had had enough of academic training. The Paris Salon refused his picture *The White Girl* in 1859, but when he exhibited it at the Salon des Refuses it created a sensation. Soon afterward Whistler settled in the Chelsea district of London, where his eccentricities made him one of the most talked-of characters in London. He named his pictures after musical arrangements, and framed them in colors to set them off to best advantage. When exhibiting them even the gallery and the liveries of attendants had to harmonize in color. He enjoyed making enemies, believing it helped to make him famous. His contemporary, Degas, called him a humbug and a self-advertising trickster. Of his having chosen a butterfly as his emblem, Oscar Wilde said derisively: "He should have chosen a wasp." Ruskin accused him of throwing a pot of paint in the public's face. But with all his peculiarities, Whistler was a hard worker, turning out, besides his paintings, nearly 400 etchings and about 150 lithographs.

At the peak of his fame, when he was fifty-four, Whistler married a widow, Mrs. Beatrix Godwin. The French government bought his *Portrait of the Artist's Mother*, painted in 1865 under the title of *An Arrangement in Grey and Black*. By 1900 his health began to fail and he traveled in Italy and Holland. Three years later he died and was buried at Chiswick beside his wife, who had died in 1896, and the mother who had inspired his most famous painting.

The model for *The Little White Girl* (page 23) was Joanna Hefferman, an Irish girl who was Whistler's companion (and probably his mistress) for many years. She called herself Mrs. Abbott. When Swinburne saw the picture he wrote the following:

> "I cannot tell what pleasures
> Or what pains were,
> What pale new loves and treasures
> New Years will bear
> What beam will fall, what shower,
> What grief or joy for dower,
> But one thing knows the flower, the flower is fair."

Whistler titled this painting *Symphony in White No. II* and painted it one year before the famous *Mother*. Arthur Studd, one of Whistler's few personal friends, bought it, later (in 1919) gave it to the National Gallery in London, where it now hangs.

GRANT WOOD
(Born 1892)

FROM PARIS, WHERE HE SPORTED PINK WHISKERS and a Basque beret, to blue denim overalls in Iowa, is Grant Wood's career in brief outline. And it is the story of an American who has found himself.

Grant Wood was born in Anamosa, Iowa. His family was rigidly Quaker and of his father it is said he once returned a copy of *Grimm's Fairy Tales* to the giver, saying: "We Quakers can read only the true things."

The artist's father died when Grant Wood was ten and from then on he supported his mother and sister. They lost the farm and moved to Cedar Rapids, where Wood worked at any odd job available. Yet he managed to graduate from high school in 1910, and during the next eight years worked at metal handicraft. He was a night watchman in a Minneapolis morgue, a jeweler, and studied art in Chicago.

At twenty-three Wood was still only a handy man about town in Cedar Rapids. He bought a lot on the edge of the town for a dollar down and a dollar a month. There in a 10-by-16-foot shack, which he built himself, he lived for two years in poverty with his mother and sister. For food Grant Wood trapped rabbits and roasted them in an outdoor fireplace. In payment for assisting a contractor in the construction of two houses, he received a suburban lot. On this he borrowed money and built himself a real home. Then America entered the World War, and Wood joined the Army. With portraits of his fellow soldiers he made a few extra dollars. After the Armistice, Cedar Rapids gave him a job teaching art for seven years. And during these years he spent his summers in Paris and Italy, associated with the "neo-meditationalists," and cultivated his pink whiskers.

The post of the American Legion in Cedar Rapids commissioned him in 1928 to design a memorial window in stained glass. He went to Munich for two years to learn about stained glass. The window was never erected for upon his return someone claimed insult to the American flag and to American workmen because Wood had the window done in Germany. The local D.A.R. entered the fray, and after this he painted his famous picture *Daughters of Revolution* (page 66).

But all this time he was eager to show his people that he could paint like a European. His Iowa landscapes looked like the south of France. His pictures sold and he was accepted as a painter. His advice was sought for home improvements and his friends paid for it. Then in a Munich museum he became fascinated by the early German masters. The detailed characterizations of simple folk suggested to him the stern-faced farmers of Iowa. Returning to Cedar Rapids, he painted *John B. Turner, Pioneer*, and after that the portrait of his mother, *Woman With Plants* (page 67). Next came *American Gothic* (page 65), the picture that made him famous. It was purchased by the Chicago Art Institute for $300. Iowa howled that he slandered its womanhood. They screamed that he held them up to ridicule. But Grant Wood from then on was known as America's "Painter of the Soil."

Grant Wood has painted very few pictures since *American Gothic*. Today, though far from wealthy, he lives in a comfortable red brick house as Artist-in-Residence at the School of Fine Arts of the University of Iowa.

CATALOGUE OF PAINTINGS

BELLOWS, GEORGE WESLEY
Stag at Sharkey's (Page 42)—Oil on canvas—36¼" x 48¼"—Painted in 1907—Purchased by the Cleveland Museum of Art from The Hinman B. Hurlbut Collection in 1922.

BENTON, THOMAS HART
The Jealous Lover of Lone Green Valley (Page 68)—Tempera on tempera board—53" x 42"—Painted in 1930—Artist's collection—Courtesy Associated American Artists.
T. P. and Jake (Page 70)—Tempera on tempera board—31" x 48"—Painted in 1937—Artist's collection—Courtesy Associated American Artists.
Pussy Cat and Roses (Page 70)—Tempera on tempera board—20" x 24"—Painted in 1939—Artist's collection—Courtesy Associated American Artists.
Persephone (Page 69)—Tempera on tempera board—55" x 72"—Painted in 1939—Artist's collection—Price $12,000—Courtesy Associated American Artists.
Huck Finn and Nigger Jim (Page 70)—Part of $16,000 45,000 square ft. mural in State House at Jefferson City, Missouri.

BIDDLE, GEORGE
Tenement (Page 102)—Fresco—10′ 6″ x 13′ 6″—Completed in August 1936. Biddle was paid $2,400 for the fresco—Department of Justice Building, Washington, D. C.—Courtesy Treasury Department, Section of Fine Arts.

BILLINGS, HENRY
Arrest No. 2—(Page 103)—Oil and tempera on gesso panel—18" x 26"—Painted in 1937—Artist's collection—Price $400:

BINGHAM, GEORGE CALEB
Daniel Boone Escorting a Band of Pioneers into the Western Country (Page 18)—Oil on canvas—36½" x 50"—Painted in 1851—Owned by Washington University, St. Louis, Missouri, a gift of Nathaniel Philips on November 18, 1890.
The Verdict of the People (Page 19)—Oil on canvas—46" x 65"—Painted in 1854-55—Given to the St. Louis Mercantile Library Association by John H. Beach.

BLANCH, ARNOLD
Basket and Fruit (Page 151)—Oil on canvas—24" x 43"—First painted in 1933, repainted in 1938—Price $500—Courtesy Associated American Artists.

BLUME, PETER
Parade (Page 106)—Oil on canvas—49¼" x 56⅜"—Painted in 1930—Owned by the Museum of Modern Art, a gift of Mrs. John D. Rockefeller, Jr.

BLYTHE, DAVID G.
General Doubleday Crossing the Potomac (Page 18)—Oil on canvas—30¼" x 40"—Painted between 1863 and 1865—Given to the National Museum of Baseball by a benefactor.

BOHROD, AARON
Landscape near Chicago (Page 104)—Oil on composition panel—24" x 32"—Price $300—Painted in 1934—Artist's collection.

BOUCHÉ, LOUIS
Mural Assistant (Page 150)—Oil on canvas—35" x 49"—Painted in 1938—Price $750—Artist's collection—Courtesy Kraushaar Art Gallery.

BRACKMAN, ROBERT
Arrangement, Life and Still Life (Page 149)—Oil on canvas—42" x 52"—Painted in 1937—Price $2,000—Courtesy The Wilmington Society of the Fine Arts, Delaware Art Center.

BROCKMAN, ANN
Nude (Page 148)—Oil on canvas—16" x 20"—Painted in 1937—Artist's collection—Price $250—Courtesy William Macbeth Gallery.

BROOK, ALEXANDER
Katharine Hepburn (Page 152)—Oil on canvas—73¾" x 34"—Painted in 1938—Owned by Katharine Hepburn.

BURCHFIELD, CHARLES E.
Six O'Clock (Page 47)—Water color on water-color paper—32½" x 38⅝"—Painted in 1936—Insurance value $3,000—Purchased for the Syracuse Museum from the Jennie Dickson Buck Fund.
Over the Dam (Page 46)—Water color on water-color paper—21" x 30"—Painted in 1936—Price paid, about $750—Owned by Miss Katharine Cornell.

CADMUS, PAUL
Coney Island (Page 100)—Oil on canvas—36" x 40"—Painted in 1934—Owned by Dr. J. R. Stark—Courtesy Midtown Galleries.

CARROLL, JOHN
White Lace (Page 154)—Oil on canvas—30" x 39¾"—Painted in 1935—Owned by The Toledo Museum of Art.

CHADWICK
Placer Mining (Page 18)—Oil on canvas—25" x 30"—Painted in 1854—Owned by Stephen C. Clark.

COLMAN, SAMUEL
Emigrant Train (Page 18)—Oil on canvas—16" x 30"—Painted in 1870—Owned by Mr. Hall Park McCullough.

CORBINO, JON
Flood Refugees (Page 45)—Oil on canvas—40" x 64"—Painted in 1938—Artist's collection—Courtesy William Macbeth Gallery.

CRAWFORD, RALSTON
Overseas Highway (Page 126)—Oil on canvas—28" x 45"—Painted in 1938—Owned by John Glen Sample—Price $600—Courtesy Boyer Gallery.

CURRY, JOHN STEUART
Baptism in Kansas (Page 73)—Oil on canvas—40" x 50"—Painted in 1928—Purchased by the Whitney Museum of American Art (1931).
Circus Elephants (Page 72)—Oil on canvas—25" x 36"—Painted in 1932—Owned by Mrs. Hendrick Eustis—Courtesy Walker Galleries.
Tornado over Kansas (Page 71)—Oil on canvas—48" x 63"—Painted in 1929—Owned by the Hackley Art Gallery, Muskegon, Michigan—Price $3,000.
Line Storm (Page 72)—Oil and tempera on panel—30" x 48"—Painted in 1934—Owned by Mrs. Sidney Howard—Courtesy Walker Galleries.

DAVIS, GLADYS ROCKMORE
The Pink Skirt (Page 148)—Oil on canvas—30" x 40"—Painted in 1938—Artist's collection—Price $1,500.

EAKINS, THOMAS
Max Schmitt in a Single Scull (Page 22)—Oil on canvas—32¼" x 46¼"—Painted in 1871—Purchased by the Metropolitan Museum of Art from the Alfred N. Punnett Fund in 1934.

ETNIER, STEPHEN
Adolescence (Page 130)—Oil on canvas—36" x 50"—Painted in 1937—Artist's collection—Courtesy The Milch Galleries.

FARNSWORTH, JERRY
The Dancer (Page 148)—Oil on canvas—36" x 43"—Painted in 1936—Artist's collection—Courtesy Grand Central Art Galleries.

CATALOGUE OF PAINTINGS

FLANNERY, VAUGHN
The Maryland Hunt (Page 130)—Oil over tempera on canvas
—54" x 72"—Painted 1937-38—Artist's collection.

FORD, LAUREN
The Country Doctor (Page 78)—Oil on canvas—71" x 53¼"—
Painted in 1935-37—Price paid for painting, $2,000—Given to
the Canajoharie Museum by Mr. Bartlett Arkell.

FULWIDER, EDWIN L.
Dead Head (Page 76)—Oil on board—30" x 38"—Painted in
1938—Artist's collection—Price $500.

GANSO, EMIL
Bearsville Meadows (Page 128)—Oil on canvas—20" x 30"—
Painted in 1938—Artist's collection—Courtesy Weyhe Gallery.

GROPPER, WILLIAM
The Senate (Page 104)—Oil on canvas—25" x 33"—Painted in
1935—Collection of the Museum of Modern Art.

HOGUE, ALEXANDRE
Drouth-Stricken Area (Page 75)—Oil on canvas—30" x 42"—
Painted in 1935—Artist's collection—Courtesy Boyer Galleries—
Price $1500.

HOMER, WINSLOW
Prisoners from the Front (Page 24)—Oil on canvas—24" x 38"—
Painted in 1866—Given to the Metropolitan Museum of Art by
Mrs. Frank B. Porter in 1922.

The Gulf Stream (Page 24)—Oil on canvas—28⅛" x 49⅛"—
Painted in 1899—Purchased by the Metropolitan Museum of Art
from the Wolfe Fund in 1906.

HOPPER, EDWARD
House by the Railroad (Page 123)—Oil on canvas—24" x 29½"
—Painted in 1925—Owned by the Museum of Modern Art, a gift
from Stephen C. Clark.

Light House at Two Lights (Page 124)—Oil on canvas—29" x
43"—Painted in 1929—Owned by Mr. and Mrs. Samuel A.
Tucker.

HURD, PETER
Boy from the Plains (Page 76)—Egg tempera on prepared board
—23½" x 24"—Painted in 1938—Price $400—Owned by Roy
Neuberger.

The Dry River (Page 77)—Egg tempera on prepared board—
41½" x 48"—Owned by Mr. and Mrs. Daniel Longwell.

INNESS, GEORGE
Peace and Plenty (Pages 20 and 21)—Oil on canvas—77⅝" x
112⅜"—Painted in 1865—Given to the Metropolitan Museum of
Art by G. A. Hearn in 1894.

JOHNSON, EASTMAN
Old Kentucky Home (Page 19)—Oil on canvas—36" x 45"—
Painted in 1859—Owned by The New York Public Library—a
bequest.

KANE, JOHN
Turtle Creek Valley (Page 101)—Oil on canvas—34" x 44"—
Painted in 1932—Owned by Mr. and Mrs. Henry R. Luce.

KLITGAARD, GEORGINA
View of Kingston (Page 128)—Oil on canvas—40" x 50"—
Painted in 1936—Artist's collection—Courtesy Frank K. M.
Rehn, Inc.

KROLL, LEON
Figure Outdoors (Page 151)—Oil on canvas—26" x 42"—Painted
in 1937—Artist's collection—Courtesy The Milch Gallery.

KUNIYOSHI, YASUO
Objects on Sofa (Page 150)—Oil on canvas—35" x 59"—Painted
in 1933—Artist's collection—Courtesy The Downtown Gallery.

LAHEY, RICHARD
My Wife (Page 150)—Oil on canvas—42½" x 84"—Painted in
1937—Artist's collection—Courtesy Kraushaar Art Galleries.

LANING, EDWARD
The Corn Dance (Page 74)—Oil on canvas—30" x 40"—Painted
in 1937—Price $800—Courtesy Midtown Galleries.

LEE, DORIS
Noon (Page 48)—Oil on canvas—28½" x 40½"—Painted in 1935
—Artist's collection—Courtesy Walker Galleries.

LIE, JONAS
Old Smuggler's Cove (Page 129)—Oil on canvas—30" x 45"—
Painted in 1938—Owned by Paul B. Sawyer—Courtesy Grand
Central Art Galleries.

LOCKWOOD, WARD
Corner Grocery, Taos (Page 76)—Oil and tempera on gesso
panel—36" x 48"—Painted in 1938—Artist's collection—Price
$1,200.

LUCIONI, LUIGI
Vermont Classic (Page 101)—Oil on canvas—42" x 20"—Painted
in 1934—Artist's collection—Price $1,800.

McCRADY, JOHN
Swing Low, Sweet Chariot (Page 99)—Oil on canvas—37" x 50"
—Painted in 1937—Purchased from the Eliza McMillan Fund by
the City Art Museum of St. Louis—Price $850.

MARSH, REGINALD
Transfer of Mail from Liner to Tugboat (Page 80) and *Sorting
Mail* (Page 80)—Fresco—Each 13' 6" x 7'—Completed in Febru-
ary 1936—Post Office Department Building, Washington, D. C.—
He was paid $1,500 for each fresco—Courtesy Treasury Depart-
ment, Section of Fine Arts.

High Yaller (Page 81)—Tempera on gesso—18" x 24"—Painted
in 1934—Owned by Mr. and Mrs. John S. Sheppard.

MATTSON, HENRY
Night and the Sea (Page 127)—Oil on canvas—38" x 58"—
Painted in 1938 — Artist's collection — Courtesy Frank K. M.
Rehn, Inc.

O'KEEFFE, GEORGIA
White Barn (Page 124)—Oil on canvas—12" x 30"—Painted in
1932—Artist's collection—Courtesy An American Place.

PALMER, WILLIAM C.
Controlled Medicine (Page 104)—Oil on canvas—6' 9" x 9' 6"—
Completed in 1937—Acquired by Queens General Hospital, Long
Island, New York—Courtesy Midtown Galleries and Federal Art
Project.

PEIRCE, WALDO
Maine Trotting Race (Page 78)—Oil on canvas—35" x 46"—
Painted in 1936—Artist's collection—Courtesy Midtown Gal-
leries.

POOR, HENRY VARNUM
*TVA Worker and Family, Pleading the Gold Case, Custom House
Workers, Surveying New Lands* (Page 82)—Fresco—All 36" x
13' 6"—Completed in September 1936—He was paid $600 for
each fresco—Department of Justice Building, Washington, D. C.
—Courtesy Treasury Department, Section of Fine Arts.

CATALOGUE OF PAINTINGS

REINDEL, EDNA
New England Harbor (Page 79)—Oil on canvas—28" x 32"—Painted in 1932—Price paid for painting, $300—Owned by Mr. David Levins.

RYDER, ALBERT PINKHAM
Death on a Pale Horse (Page 22)—Oil on canvas—28¼" x 35¼"—Painted about 1910—Purchased by the Cleveland Museum of Art from the J. H. Wade Fund in 1928.

SALMON, ROBERT W.
Boston Harbor—Long and Central Wharves (Page 18)—Oil on wood—16¼" x 24"—Owned by Henry R. Dalton (inherited)—Insured for $1,000.

SAMPLE, PAUL
Janitor's Holiday (Page 75)—Oil on canvas—26" x 40"—Painted in 1936—Purchased by the Metropolitan Museum of Art from the A. H. Hearn Fund in 1937.

SARGENT, JOHN SINGER
The Wyndham Sisters (Page 41)—Oil on canvas—115" x 84⅛"—Painted in 1900—Purchased by the Metropolitan Museum of Art from the Wolfe Fund in 1927 for $90,000.

SHEELER, CHARLES
City Interior (Page 126)—Oil on prepared board—22" x 27"—Painted in 1936—Purchased by the Worcester Art Museum from bequest of Elizabeth M. Sawyer in memory of Johnathan and Elizabeth M. Sawyer—Courtesy Worcester Art Museum.

SLOAN, JOHN
Sunday, Women Drying Their Hair (Page 43)—Oil on canvas—25½" x 31½"—Painted about 1914—Purchased by the Addison Gallery, Andover, Massachusetts.

Wake of the Ferry No. 2 (Page 44)—Oil on canvas—26" x 32"—Painted in 1907—Owned by Phillips Memorial Gallery.

SOYER, RAPHAEL
Doctor's Office (Page 105)—Oil on canvas—27½" x 23½"—Painted in 1938—Artist's collection.

SPEICHER, EUGENE
The Blue Necklace (Page 148)—Oil on canvas—33⅛" x 40⅛"—Painted in 1937—Owned by the Toledo Museum of Art.

Katharine Cornell as Candida (Page 153)—Oil on canvas—84" x 44½"—Painted in 1925-1926—Owned by the Museum of Modern Art, a gift of Miss Katharine Cornell.

TAUBES, FREDERIC
Rehearsal (Page 147)—Oil on canvas—50" x 40"—Painted in 1937—Owned by Mr. George Gross—Courtesy Midtown Galleries.

TRUMBULL, JOHN
The Surrender of Lord Cornwallis (Page 17)—Oil on canvas—21⅛" x 30⅝"—Painted in 1786-87—Purchased from Colonel Trumbull in 1831, an item in the collection acquired from him for a thousand-dollar-a-year annuity—Owned by the Yale University Gallery of Fine Arts.

WAUGH, FREDERICK J.
The Big Water (Page 125)—Oil on especially prepared panel—48" x 60"—Painted in 1937—Owned by Ernest E. Quantrell—Courtesy Grand Central Art Galleries.

WEST, BENJAMIN
The Death of Wolfe (Page 17)—Oil on canvas—60½" x 84"—Painted in 1770—Given to the National Gallery, Ottawa, Ontario, Canada, by the Duke of Westminster.

WHISTLER, JAMES MCNEILL
The Little White Girl (Page 23)—Oil on canvas—29½" x 19½"—Painted in 1864—Purchased by Arthur Studd and, in 1919, given to the National Gallery, London.

WOOD, GRANT
American Gothic (Page 65)—Oil on panel board—29⅞" x 25"—Painted in 1930—Owned by the Chicago Art Institute—Courtesy Associated American Artists.

Daughters of Revolution (Page 66)—Oil on panel board—20" x 40"—Painted in 1932—Owned by Edward G. Robinson—Courtesy Associated American Artists.

Woman with Plants (Page 67)—Oil on panel board—20½" x 17½"—Painted in 1929—Owned by the Cedar Rapids Fine Arts Association—Courtesy Associated American Artists.

The text of this book is set in Centaur and Arrighi, the display in Weiss. The color illustrations were printed by letter-press from plates originally manufactured by the R. R. Donnelley & Sons Company for Life. The volume was designed by Avery R. Fisher of Dodd, Mead & Company.

The composition was done by American Book-Stratford Press under the supervision of Ralph M. Duenewald, the printing and binding by The Haddon Craftsmen, Inc.